the BOOKS of MAGIC

The Burning Girl

John Ney Rieber
Peter Gross
writers

Peter Snejbjerg
Peter Gross
artists

Nathan Eyring
Sherilyn Van Valkenburgh
colorists

Richard Starkings &
Comicraft/LA
letterer

Michael Wm. Kaluta
cover art–issues 33–40

Sherilyn Van Valkenburgh
cover art–issue 41

Neil Gaiman
consultant

Timothy Hunter and
the Books of Magic
created by
Neil Gaiman and John Bolton

The Books of Magic: The Burning Girl

Published by DC Comics.

Originally published in single magazine form as
THE BOOKS OF MAGIC 33-41.

DC Comics, 1700 Broadway, New York, NY 10019
A division of Warner Bros. -
A Time Warner Entertainment Company
Printed in Canada. First Printing.
ISBN: 1-56389-619-2
Cover illustration by Michael Wm. Kaluta.
Publication design by Addie Blaustein.

The Story So Far

Tim Hunter was an ordinary London boy—until he learned he had the potential to become the world's greatest mage. But now Tim has left his family and home to wander across America, and despite his gifts, this special teenager finds himself lost and rootless.

Molly O'Reilly, Tim's girlfriend, has been cursed by Queen Titania of the Faerie realm. Now Molly is trapped in Faerie; if she returns home to Earth, she will die. And while Titania has apologized for her rash actions, the curse remains—and Molly's anger burns bright.

Fate brought Tim and Molly together, and now fate has pulled them apart. But dark forces are gathering in Faerie, and soon the young lovers may meet again. . . .

Timothy Hunter was just another teen-ager -- until he learned of his destiny to become the most powerful magician of his era. Driven to his breaking point by both sorcerous pressures and everyday adolescent concerns, Tim left his London home behind and came to the United States, where he now explores the American Southwest.
CRAZY LIGHTNING HAS BEEN SMOKING THE SAME CIGAR FOR FORTY YEARS.
NOT MANY PEOPLE CAN DO THAT.
GOLDEN SHIRT SALOON
ONE OF THESE DAYS, SOMEONE IS GOING TO ASK HIM HOW HE DOES IT.
HE SURE HOPES SO, ANYWAY.
IT'S BEEN A WHILE SINCE HE HAD A GOOD BELLY-SHAKING THUNDER-LAUGH.
HE'S GOT FOUR ANSWERS READY...
...ONE FOR EACH CLAN OF THE ASKING PEOPLE.
WHAT --
-- DIDN'T YOU KNOW THAT THERE WERE FOUR CLANS OF ASKING PEOPLE?
Oh, WELL.
GUESS YOU'RE NOT FROM AROUND HERE.

HIST
RATTLE YOUR HOCKS, CHIHUAHUA KID --
I SEE WIDE OPEN SPACES. LET'S RIDE.
THE OLD SNAKE IS JUST A-FUNNING US, MONTEREY JACK.
HE'S A-GONNA HEAD US OFF AT THE PASS, I JUST KNOW IT.
JING JING
I CAN FEEL IT IN MY --
THOP
HOW MANY TIMES I GOT TO TELL YOU, KID?
I DON'T GIVE A HOOT WHAT YOU FEEL IN YOUR DOGGONE BONES.
WHAT GOES ON BETWEEN A MAN AND HIS BONES, WELL...
THAT'S BETWEEN HIM AND THE UNDERTAKER, SON.

YOU JUST KEEP TELLING YOURSELF HOW FRISKY YOU'RE GOING TO BE FEELING WHEN HIGH NOON ROLLS AROUND TOMORROW, AND YOU AND ME AIN'T HAVING TO SHOOT HOLES IN EACH OTHER AS USUAL.
THAT'LL BE REAL NICE, WON'T IT?
BUT SAY, NOW --
THAT AIN'T A SEEGAR YOU'RE A-SMOKING, IS IT?
NOPE.
THEN HOW COME I'M A-SMELLING --
RECKON IT'S TRUE WHAT THEY SAY ABOUT YOU, KID --
YOU GOT A NOSE IN THE BACK OF YOUR HEAD, SURE ENOUGH.
TIK
HOLD IT RIGHT THERE, OLD-TIMER --
TIK
YEAH --
AND DON'T YOU BE MAKING NO SUDDEN MOVES, NEITHER.
DRINK, SHERIFFS?
IT'S A LONG DRY WALK BACK TO TOWN.

CRAZY LIGHTNING ISN'T A DRINKING MAN HIMSELF.

HE ONLY KEEPS THE POISON AROUND TO BE HOSPITABLE.

WELL, KID...
RECKON HE'S GOT US OUTGUNNED.
SHIKASHISHSHI

NO --

YEP.
RECKON I'LL BE SEEING YOU BACK DOWN ON MAIN STREET, THEN...
AT HIGH NOON.

AWW, NO...

AND DON'T FORGET --
THE SCRIPT SAYS IT'S YOUR TURN TO WEAR THE BLACK HAT, THIS TIME.

NO...
NOT THE BLACK HAT, MAMA. NOT AGAIN...

PLEASE, MISTER --
LET ME GO.

I AIN'T NEVER DONE NOTHING TO YOU.
I CAN'T EVEN RIGHTLY SAY WHO YOU IS.

ALL I EVER DONE WAS WEAR THE BADGE IN A FEW OF THEM MOVING PICTURES...

WHY... ARE YOU...
... TORMENTING MY GHOST...
IN THIS T-TERRIBLE WAY?

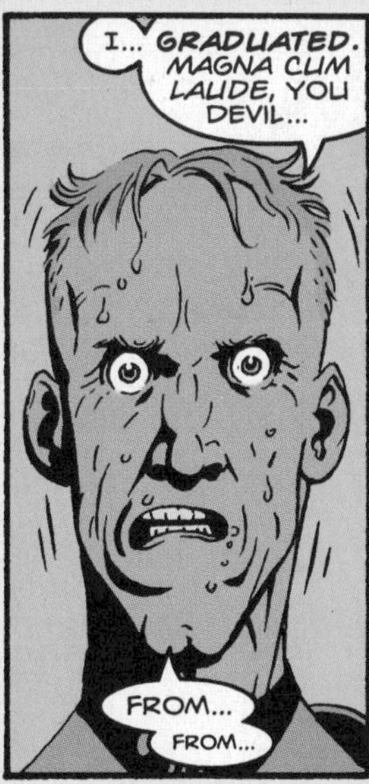
I... GRADUATED. MAGNA CUM LAUDE, YOU DEVIL...
FROM...
FROM...

FROM PRINCE-TOWN, DAGNAB IT.

YOU'RE A LONG WAY FROM PRINCETON NOW, KID.
YOU WON'T PASS HISTORY HERE UNTIL YOU'VE LEARNED IT.

WHAT ARE YOU DOING?

THOSE MEN SHOULD BE *DEAD* --
AND RESTING IN *PEACE* OR WHATEVER.

DO YOU KNOW WHAT THIS IS?
IT'S A *BOTTLE*.

NO.
IT'S A *GHOST* OF A BOTTLE.

SO?

IT'S A LOT EASIER TO MAKE GHOSTS OUT OF *PEOPLE* THAN *BOTTLES*, KID.
FOLLOW ME?

YOU'RE A *BRIT*. THIS HAS GOT NOTHING TO *DO* WITH YOU.
SO QUIT WHILE YOU'RE *AHEAD*, Huh? GET OUT OF TOWN. THERE'S NOTHING FOR YOU HERE BUT *TROUBLE*.
chhkashhshshh

THERE'S WATER, IF THAT'S A WELL DOWN THERE.
AND I'D BE DELIGHTED TO BE IN TROUBLE, IF I COULD HAVE SOMETHING TO DRINK FIRST.

Mmph.

YOU'RE OKAY, KID. DUMB AS A POST IF YOU'RE TRAVELLING WITHOUT WATER, BUT OKAY.
DRINK?
I'M FOURTEEN.

THAT'S OLD ENOUGH FOR LEMONADE.
GO AHEAD, KID.
KNOCK YOURSELF OUT, IT'S FRESH.
DON'T CALL ME KID. MY NAME IS TIM.
THAT THING WITH THE HAT ON WAS A KID.
LISTEN, KID --
SPARE ME THE ATTITUDE.

I'M CRAZY LIGHTNING.
IF I WANTED TO KNOW YOUR NAME, I'D NAME YOU.

HAH!
I DON'T KNOW ABOUT THE LIGHTNING PART, BUT YOU'RE DEFINITELY CRAZY --
IF YOU EXPECT ME TO BELIEVE THAT YOU'RE AN INDIAN.

NO -- I'M NOT AN INDIAN.
I'M A NATIVE AMERICAN.
AND YOU'RE A SMARTASS BRIT TOURIST WHO'S JUST SUCKED DOWN THE LAST OF MY LEMONADE.

GLAD WE GOT THAT SETTLED?
NOW GET LOST.

I DIDN'T MEAN TO INSULT YOU.
IT'S JUST THAT YOU DON'T LOOK LIKE AN INDIA... uh, NATIVE AMERICAN.

SATISFIED, KID?
THIS IS ME.

YOU'RE...
A RATTLE-SNAKE?
CALL ME GRAND-FATHER.
GREAT. THAT'S JUST WHAT I NEED...
ANOTHER REPTILE IN MY FAMILY TREE.
YOU HAVE A LOT TO LEARN, KID.
ON THE ROAD YOU ARE TRAVELLING, LAUGHTER IS POWER...
... BUT MOCKERY WILL GET YOU SKINNED ALIVE.
YOU'RE GOING TO DIE HERE, IF I DON'T BITE YOU AGAIN.
IS THAT WHAT YOU WANT?
N-NO.
NO, WHO?
NO, GRANDFATHER.

YOU'RE A STRANGER IN MY LAND, KID.
LET ME TELL YOU HOW THINGS WORK AROUND HERE.

YOU WANT TO SPIT VENOM? THAT'S FINE.
JUST REMEMBER...

EVENTUALLY YOU'RE GOING TO RUN INTO SOMEONE WHO'S BETTER AT IT THAN YOU ARE.

IT'S A ROAD YOU'RE ON, KID... BUT IT'S A WHEEL, TOO.
AND WHAT COMES AROUND GOES AROUND.

YOU DON'T HAVE TO TAKE MY WORD FOR IT.
ASK THE NEIGHBORS.

Ahhh... YOU KNOW NOW, DON'T YOU, KID?
I AM YOUR GRANDFATHER...
BECAUSE THERE'S A SNAKE INSIDE YOU --
-- YEAH, YOU AND THE REST OF THE VERTEBRATES.
YOU CALL IT A SPINE, BUT A SNAKE IS WHAT IT IS.
YOU'RE A LITTLE GREEN YET TO REALLY WAKE IT UP...
... BUT YOU DON'T HAVE TO WAKE THE SERPENT TO LOOK INTO ITS EYES.
SEE?
IT'S THE PART OF YOU THAT SHUNS PAIN AND SEEKS PLEASURE.
IT'S THE PART OF YOU THAT KNOWS WHEN IT'S TIME TO BACK AWAY, AND WHEN IT'S TIME TO STRIKE.
IT BREATHES FOR YOU. IT TELLS YOUR HEART TO BEAT.
IT PULLS YOUR FINGERS OUT OF THE FIRE BEFORE THEY BURN.
IT HEARS THE MESSAGES THE WORLD SENDS YOU THROUGH YOUR BODY.
IT KNOWS THE TASTE OF TIME, BUT NOT THE FEAR OF IT.

WHAT?

Oh, YOU'D BE PRICKLY, *TOO*, KID --

IF YOU'D BEEN THROUGH WHAT *I'VE* BEEN THROUGH.

SO HOW ARE YOU DOING?
I DON'T KNOW. I...

GOD, I DON'T BELIEVE THIS. I JUST SHED MY SKIN.
AND I'M SITTING HERE TALKING TO YOU LIKE NOTHING HAPPENED.

WHAT DID YOU DO TO ME?
I FEEL ALL...
SALOON

CALM?
I DON'T KNOW. SORT OF...

I'M RELAXED. A LOT MORE RELAXED THAN I OUGHT TO BE, CONSIDERING...
BUT THAT'S JUST MY BODY. MY MIND, WELL...

I GUESS IT'S RELAXED, TOO.
BUT IT'S NOTICING THINGS IN THIS WEIRD WAY.

I MEAN, I'M *LOOKING* AT THIS.

AND *USUALLY* IF I DID THAT...

I'D JUST SEE A *WEED...*

AND I *DO* STILL SEE THE WEED.

BUT NOW I SEE ITS *LEAVES,* TOO. AND THEY'RE...

YOU THINK I OUGHT TO LET THOSE GHOSTS DOWN THERE GO?
BELIEVE ME, KID --
-- THERE'S NOTHING I'D LIKE BETTER.
BUT IT'S NOT GOING TO HAPPEN UNTIL THEY UNDER-STAND.
"IT TOOK ME A WHILE TO PUT MYSELF TOGETHER, YOU KNOW? I DIDN'T REALLY CONDENSE UNTIL THE FORTIES --
" TOO LATE TO SETTLE SCORES WITH THE HAT-HEADS WHO REALLY HAD IT COMING.
"SETTLERS, YOUR HISTORY BOOKS WOULD CALL THEM.
"I'D BE MORE INCLINED TO CALL THEM UNSETTLERS, MYSELF:
"LIARS. BUTCHERS. THIEVES."

"BUT LIKE I SAID --

" I DIDN'T REALLY **COME TOGETHER** UNTIL THE FORTIES, WHEN HOLLYWOOD SET UP THIS LITTLE RESERVATION HERE.

"AND DECIDED, 'AWW, NEVER MIND **HOW** WE GOT THIS SCENERY.'

"'FORGET THE BONE AND HEART AND HISTORY BURIED **UNDER** IT.'

"'LET'S MAKE US SOME MYTHS AND SOME MONEY. YEE-**HAW**...'"

EVEN **THEN**, I MIGHT NOT HAVE HAPPENED...

... IF THE **MOVING PICTURE** COWBOYS HADN'T TURNED OUT TO BE HARDER TO LIVE WITH THAN THE **REAL** HAT-HEADS HAD BEEN.

THAT'S SAD.

BUT WHAT DOES IT HAVE TO DO WITH ME?
ME AND MY INNER SNAKE?

KID...
... YOU WANT ME TO LET THOSE GHOSTS GO?
I WANT TO LET THOSE GHOSTS GO.

IF YOU CAN FIND A SINGLE HAT-HEAD DOWN THERE WHO GIVES A FLYING BUFFALO CHIP ABOUT ANY KIND OF LIFE BUT HIS?
I'LL CUT THE WHOLE DAMN HERD LOOSE.

SO GO CLEAN UP THAT TOWN, KID.
JUST REMEMBER -- I DON'T WANT YOU HATING ME, NOW.
THE THINGS YOU SEE THEM DOING DOWN THERE? THE THINGS YOU HEAR THEM SAYING?

THEY'RE ALL THINGS THEY SAID AND DID OF THEIR OWN FREE WILL...
BACK WHEN THEY THOUGHT THEY WERE MEN.

BANG
EVENING, GENTLEMEN.
BANG
SKRUTCH
PURGATORY DRY WHISTLE SALOON
YOU'RE **NEW** IN TOWN.
YEP.
ME AND THE BOYS DON'T MUCH **COTTON** TO FOLKS BEING NEW IN TOWN.
THAT'S MIGHTY **PECULIAR,** PARDNER.
WEREN'T ***YOU AND THE BOYS*** EVER NEW IN TOWN?
WHY, YOU LOW-DOWN BACK-STABBING ***VARMINT*** --
GIT HIM, BOYS!
BANG
BANG
BANG
SHAME ON YOU.
I'VE MET ***MANTICORES*** MORE NEIGHBORLY THAN ***YOU-ALL.***

DANG.
BOYS, I RECKON WE'VE JUST BEEN INSULTED.
CREEK
THE KID --
LORDY.
A REAL ONE.

ALL RIGHT -- I'M NOT LOOKING FOR TROUBLE.
I JUST WANT TO KNOW ONE THING --
IS THERE ANYTHING IN YOUR LIFE THAT MEANS AS MUCH TO YOU AS YOU DO?

WHY, SURE... ROUNDING THINGS UP. ROPING THINGS, BRANDING THINGS --

PLAYING POKER. CHEWING T'BACCY. DRINKING --
WHOA THERE--

DON'T PAY THEM NO MIND, KID.
THEY'RE NOT REAL COWBOYS.
SKURK

REAL COWBOYS, WE RIDE AND SING, AND HAVE SHOOTOUTS AND SUCH.
BUT MOSTLY WE JUST RIDE.
RIDE WHAT?
WHERE ARE YOUR HORSES?
WHERE DID THEY GO?

YOU KNOW WHAT **HAPPENS** TO HORSES WITH **BROKEN LEGS,** KID?

BANG, THAT'S WHAT HAPPENS.

REFRESHED, THE BOY CONTINUES ON HIS WAY.

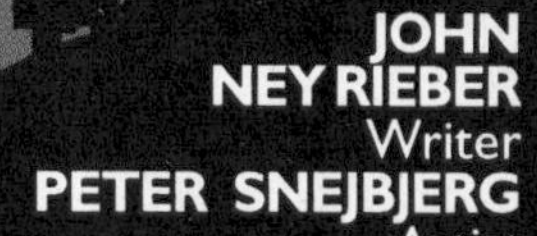

JOHN NEY RIEBER Writer
PETER SNEJBJERG Artist
NATHAN EYRING Colorist
RS/COMICRAFT Letters
NEIL GAIMAN Consultant JULIE ROTTENBERG Editor
TIMOTHY HUNTER and the BOOKS OF MAGIC created by NEIL GAIMAN and JOHN BOLTON

Young Timothy Hunter, destined to become the world's greatest mage, came to America hoping to escape the sorcerous and personal woes that plagued him in England. While he explores the American Southwest, his ex-girlfriend Molly remains trappped in Faerie, suffering the effects of Queen Titania's curse, and caught at the center of an all-out war.

FAERIE.

THIS WAS *WAR.*

Fire & Sugar & Spice

Rites of Passage Part 8

John Ney Rieber
Writer
Peter Snejbjerg
Artist
Nathan Eyring
Colorist

Richard Starkings & Comicraft
Letters
Neil Gaiman
Consultant
Julie Rottenberg
Editor

Timothy Hunter & The Books of Magic
Created by
Neil Gaiman
and
John Bolton

HUNTSMEN --

HARRY HER DOWN.

BRING ME HER ***HEART*** WHEN THE CHASE IS DONE.
GLADLY, MY QUEEN.
COME, LADS --

LADY, WAIT --

FWOOSH

SHE IS *HERE,* MY HUNTSMAN...

SOMEWHERE...

CRACKLE

HOW MANY OF YOU SILVER BOYS WILL STAY TO GUARD HER?

HALF?
LOVELY.

ONE, TWO, THREE...
WHAT DO YOU SAY, BOYS?
LET'S TAKE THOSE LONG BOWS OF YOURS INTO THE WOODS.

FOUR, FIVE, SIX...
WHAT'S THE MATTER WITH YOU BOYS?
HAVEN'T YOU EVER CHASED A BURNING GIRL BEFORE?

WHICH ONE OF YOU BOYS HAS GOT THAT PRETTY SILVER BOX?
TO PUT MY HEART IN.
TO GIVE TO THE BITCH.
MY HEART...

Oh, IT'S A LOVELY BOX, BOYS.
WORTHY OF A QUEEN, I'M SURE.

CLICK
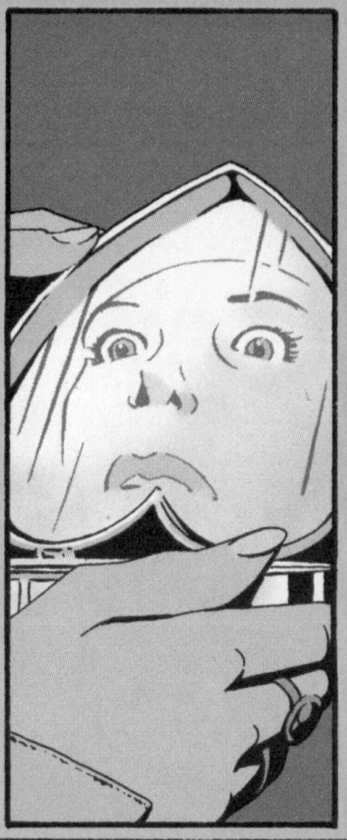
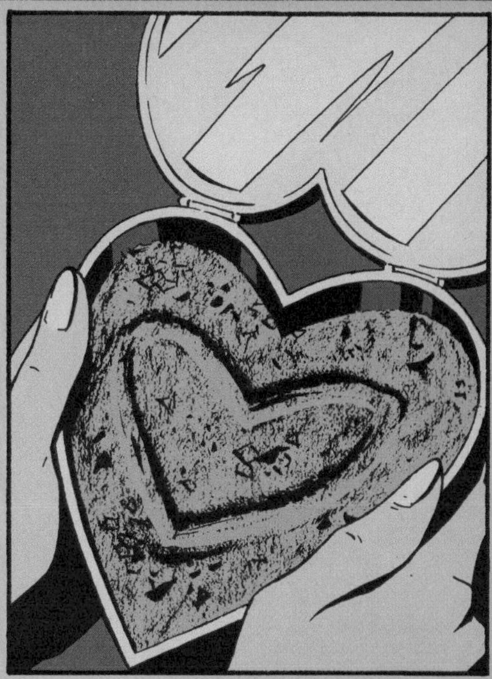

TAK

SHE LEFT THIS AT MY FEET.
I DID NOT SEE HER COME OR GO.

I *FEAR* HER, SELWYN.
NOT FOR HER *POWER*, INEXPLICABLE AND TERRIBLE AS IT MAY BE...
BUT BECAUSE SHE GIVES ME *TRUTH*.

I AM TO BLAME FOR THIS...
ALL OF THIS. DO YOU UNDERSTAND?

SHE IS LIKE A *MIRROR*, SELWYN. *TWISTED*, YES, BUT SO *BRIGHT* --
AND IT IS MY OWN FACE SHE IS SHOWING ME.

SHE DOES *NOTHING* TO ME BUT WHAT I HAVE DONE TO *HER*...
OR *SOUGHT* TO DO, THE STARS FORGIVE ME...

I TOOK HER WORLD AWAY FROM HER. SHE DESPOILS ME OF MINE.
I GAVE THE ORDER FOR A HEART TO BE PLACED WITHIN THIS BOX. SHE RETURNS IT TO ME, FILLED...

SHE TEACHES ME THE KIND OF QUEEN I AM.

DO YOU BEAR FIRE ALONG THE ROAD?

AT THE QUEEN'S COMMAND, NO FIRE MAY PASS US.

ARE YOU THE FIRE-GIRL -- MOLLY O REILLY?

WE SHALL WRAP AND QUENCH YOU, IF YOU BLAZE...

tchah!

Ahhh...

IT IS BUT A BEAST.

THE GOBLIN MARKET.
FOR A PRICE, FOR THE ASKING...
OR, MORE PERILOUSLY, FOR THE TAKING...
WHAT MAY NOT BE FOUND HERE?
WONDERS BY THE BUSHEL, NEPENTHE BY THE BOTTLE...
DARK WISHES THAT CLATTER TO LIFE AT THE TURN OF A KEY...
MUSIC MADE FLESH, DANCING IN SWIRLS OF SILK, AND FLESH MADE MUSIC, SKIRLING.

FERMENTING IN CASKS, PREENING IN CAGES...
SLEEPING IN PAVILIONS, WEEPING IN SACKS...
GUTTERING IN EYES AND SWORD-SHEATHS AND OUTSTRETCHED HANDS...
HERE ONE MAY FIND MUCH TO FASCINATE THE SENSES AND THE HEART...
AND PRECIOUS LITTLE TO SATISFY THEM.
HORSES DO NOT OFTEN COME HERE OF THEIR OWN FREE WILL.

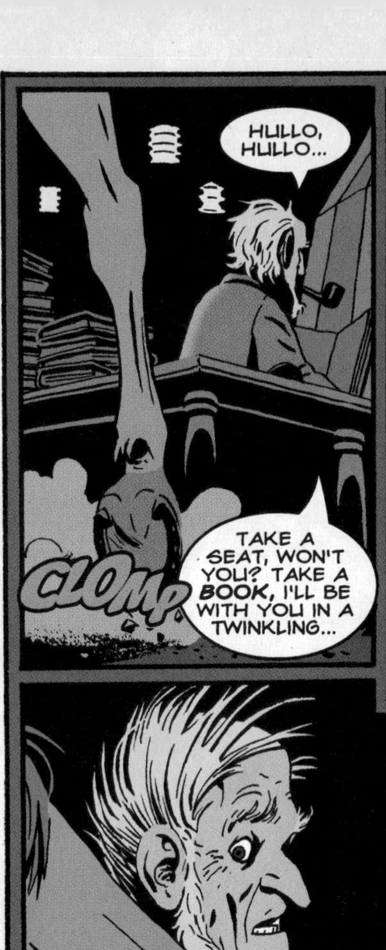
HULLO, HULLO...
TAKE A SEAT, WON'T YOU? TAKE A BOOK, I'LL BE WITH YOU IN A TWINKLING...
CLOMP

CLOMP
PEACE, FRIEND!

I SUFFER FROM A PECULIAR AFFLICTION.
ONCE I HAVE BEGUN TO READ A SENTENCE, I CANNOT CEASE UNTIL I REACH ITS END...

CHUFF

TAIK?

TAIK, WHAT DO YOU THINK YOU ARE DOING, WANDERING AROUND WITH A MANE AND TAIL?

AN ATROCIOUSLY UNKEMPT MANE AND TAIL, IF I MAY SAY SO.
PRINCE, YOUR MOTHER WOULD SIMPLY CURL UP HER TOES AND DIE IF SHE--

SHE NEVER...
SHE DID?

AND YOU'VE A STONE IN YOUR HOOF AS WELL?
Oh, DEAR...
AHUM...

FIVE GOOD GOLD CROWNS FOR THE LITERATE HORSE, MASTER!
SIX, IF HE CAN PLOW AS CLEVER AS HE WRITES --

THIS, MY FRIENDS...
IS A PRIVATE CONVERSATION.

MY APOLOGIES, PRINCE --
PEOPLE DO BEHAVE QUITE ODDLY AT THE MARKET.
THEY SEEM TO BELIEVE THAT EVERYTHING'S FOR SALE.
IT'S SOMETHING THE WARDENS PUT IN THE WATER, I SHOULDN'T WONDER.
WELL, LET US DO SOMETHING ABOUT THE STONE IN YOUR HOOF, AND THEN WE WILL SEE WHAT CAN BE DONE TO RESTORE YOUR PROPER SHAPE.
UNLESS YOU ARE TERRIBLY HUNGRY, IN WHICH CASE I COULD TURN YOU OUT TO GRAZE FOR A BIT...
THERE.
I HAVE NEVER LIKED TITANIA, YOU KNOW. SHE'S GREEN.
WHAT KIND OF COLOR IS THAT FOR A QUEEN TO BE, I ASK YOU?
Hmmm...
BUT SPEAKING OF GREEN, AND GREENERY...
HAVE YOU TRIED EATING ROSES?
NOW, IF TITANIA HAD MADE A MULE OF YOU, EATING DAMASK ROSEBLOSSOMS WOULD DISSOLVE THE ENCHANTMENT...
BUT AS YOU ARE MANIFESTLY NOT A MULE, PERHAPS WE OUGHT TO...
Oh, BOTHER --
PERHAPS IT WOULD BE BEST IF WE SIMPLY RETURNED TO THE MARKET, Eh?
WE WILL FIND THE NEAREST FLORIST, AND START EATING.

Hmmm...
THIS WAY, TAIK.
I AM ALMOST CERTAIN THAT I SAW A FLOWER-SELLER SOMEWHERE OVER HERE...

KRASH
OR WAS IT OVER HERE..?

TCHAH!

SHE IS BUT A SMALL FIRE, AFTER ALL.
TOO SMALL TO FEED US BOTH?
LET US SEE.

NEIGHHHEIGH

PRINCE! GET AWAY FROM THEM!
THEY'LL SMOTHER YOU, YOU LUNKHEAD!

GO AWAY!
YOU'RE GOING TO GET HURT, YOU STUPID HORSE, I DON'T WANT YOU TO GET HURT --

NO--! I CAN'T GET ON YOU, YOU IDIOT --
DON'T YOU UNDERSTAND?

I CAN'T TOUCH YOU.
I'LL BURN YOU.
CAN'T YOU SEE?
I'M NOT ME ANYMORE --

HEY --

THAT'S MY *FOOT!*

THAT WAS A DIRTY TRICK.
HOW'D YOU LIKE IT IF I --
MY GOD...
I'M NOT SURE HOW YOU DID THAT...
BUT WHAT ARE YOU DOING FOR THE REST OF MY LIFE?

ROSES. PFFF.
IF I LIVE TO BE AS OLD AS MYRVYN, I WILL NEVER EAT ANOTHER ROSE.

'TIS ODD...

HAVE I BEEN WEARING THESE CLOTHES FOR A HUNDRED YEARS, OR HAVE I NOT?

AT LEAST THEY DO NOT SMELL OF HORSE.

Ohhh, MOTHER...

YOU HAVE MUCH TO ANSWER FOR, I THINK.

NEIGHHHEIGH

PRINCE?

HEY --

WHERE'S **PRINCE?** WHERE DID HE **GO?**

HE STRAYED DOWN TO THE **RIVER,** LADY. TO DRINK AND TO BATHE, AND...

Oh, TO **SPLASH,** I BELIEVE.

AND THEN HE DID RETURN HERE...

TO SIT, AND WAIT FOR YOU TO **WAKE.**

Oh.

I SEE...

I THINK.

Young Timothy Hunter, destined to become the world's greatest mage, came to America hoping to escape the sorcerous and personal woes that plagued him in England. While he wanders around the American Southwest, his ex-girlfriend Molly remains trapped in Faerie, suffering the effects of Queen Titania's curse. And now the horse Prince, one of Molly's few friends in Faerie, has just revealed himself to be a boy -- and, in fact, a real prince.

Rites of Passage Part NINE

Appearances

John Ney Rieber
Writer

Peter Snejbjerg
Artist

Nathan Eyring
Colorist

Richard Starkings & Comicraft/LA
Letters

Neil Gaiman
Consultant

Julie Rottenberg
Editor

Timothy Hunter & The Books of Magic
Created by
Neil Gaiman
and
John Bolton

I DO NOT KNOW WHAT I WOULD DO *WITHOUT YOU,* SELWYN.
I BELIEVE THAT I WOULD GO *MAD.*

WHY HAVE YOU REMAINED BY MY SIDE?
YOU *ALONE,* OF ALL THOSE IN WHOM I ONCE PLACED MY *TRUST?*

I --

LADY, IT IS *MELANCHOLY* WHICH TINTS YOUR WORLD SO DARK.
SURELY THERE ARE *MANY* BESIDES MYSELF WHO HAVE NOT FORSAKEN YOU -- LORD *AUBERON,* FOR ONE --
HUSH.

YOU ARE HERE AND *I* AM HERE.
AND WHERE ARE THESE *OTHERS* YOU SPEAK OF?

I DO NOT *BLAME THEM,* SELWYN.
I BETRAYED *THEIR* TRUST ERE THEY BETRAYED MINE.
IT IS NOT A *QUEEN* I HAVE BEEN TO *ANY* OF THEM...
LEAST OF ALL TO THE KING.

BUT I AM RESOLVED NOW TO RULE WITH WISDOM, AS BEFITS A QUEEN OF FAERIE.
THIS VERY DAY I SHALL CONSULT THE BOOK.
THE BOOK?
AYE -- THE BOOK OF A SINGLE PAGE.

LADY --
LADY, IS THIS WISDOM?

HUSH.
IT IS NOT YOUR COUNSEL I NEED NOW, MY DARLING.

ELSEWHERE.
MADNESS!

AIEE!
WHO WOULD DARE HANG SUCH A VILE THING, HERE IN THE QUEEN'S GREEN GARDEN?

WHAT CAN IT SIGNIFY?
IT EXHALES A FEARSOME TAINT...

Ohhh...
IT WREAKS A BANE-WEAVE... OF THREE HEART-WRACKS AND A RUIN...
UPON THE FEY GIRL?

THIS IS...
THIS IS WRONG...

IT WAS NO DEED OF HERS THAT MADE HER WHAT SHE IS.
WHY SHOULD SHE BE REVILED AND CURSED THUS?
TAK
SHE HAS BURNED A BLACK SWATH THROUGH THE REALM, THIS I KNOW --
-- BUT I CANNOT FAULT HER FOR IT.
SHE WAS CONTENT TO WORK AND SING HERE, AND THINK BRAVE SOLITARY THOUGHTS...
UNTIL HER BOND WITH THE WORLD OF HER BIRTH WAS BROKEN...
AND SHE KNEW THAT SHE MUST DWELL FOREVER IN FAERIE, OR CRUMBLE INTO DUST...
AND WHO IS TO BLAME FOR HER GRIEF, AND FOR FAERIE'S?
WHOSE MOON-SPELL TRICKED HER INTO TASTING FAIRY FRUIT?
WHOSE MALICE KINDLED BALE-FIRE IN HER HEART?
CLAP CLAP CLAP

BRAVO, LITTLE YARROW!

DO CONTINUE...

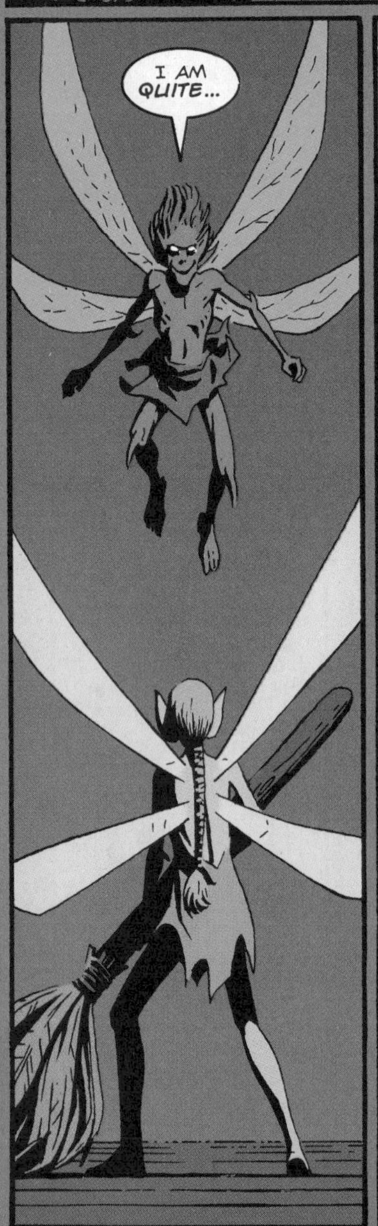
I AM *QUITE*...

INTRIGUED...

BY YOUR TALE.

ELSEWHERE.

I THINK...

YOU DO NOTHING *BUT* THINK.

ARE *ALL* MORTAL FOLK AS *CALCULATING* AS YOU?

I DO NOT KNOW WHEN LAST I SAW MY DARLING MOTHER.
AND AS TO WHY SHE GAVE ME A HORSE'S SHAPE?

SHE NEVER SAID.

MOLLY?

I HAVE ANSWERED YOU.
PERHAPS YOU HEARD?

MOLLY?

JESUS --

I CAN HEAR THEM.

I'M *HEARING THEM* AGAIN, THE VOICES...
THEY'RE *SOFT* NOW, BUT THEY'RE *THERE*...

CHRIST, I'VE GOT TO TAKE MY *MEDS*.
OR I'LL BE SEEING THINGS BEFORE YOU KNOW IT. AND --

I DON'T *HAVE* ANY.
I LEFT THEM ALL BACK IN THE *REAL* WORLD.

SHIT.
THEY'RE SAYING I SHOULD RUN.
DID YOU SAY "THEY"?
MOLLY, DO YOU HEAR VOICES?
YOU HEAR VOICES.
WHAT KIND OF VOICES?
WHAT DO THEY SAY?
DO THEY SAY?

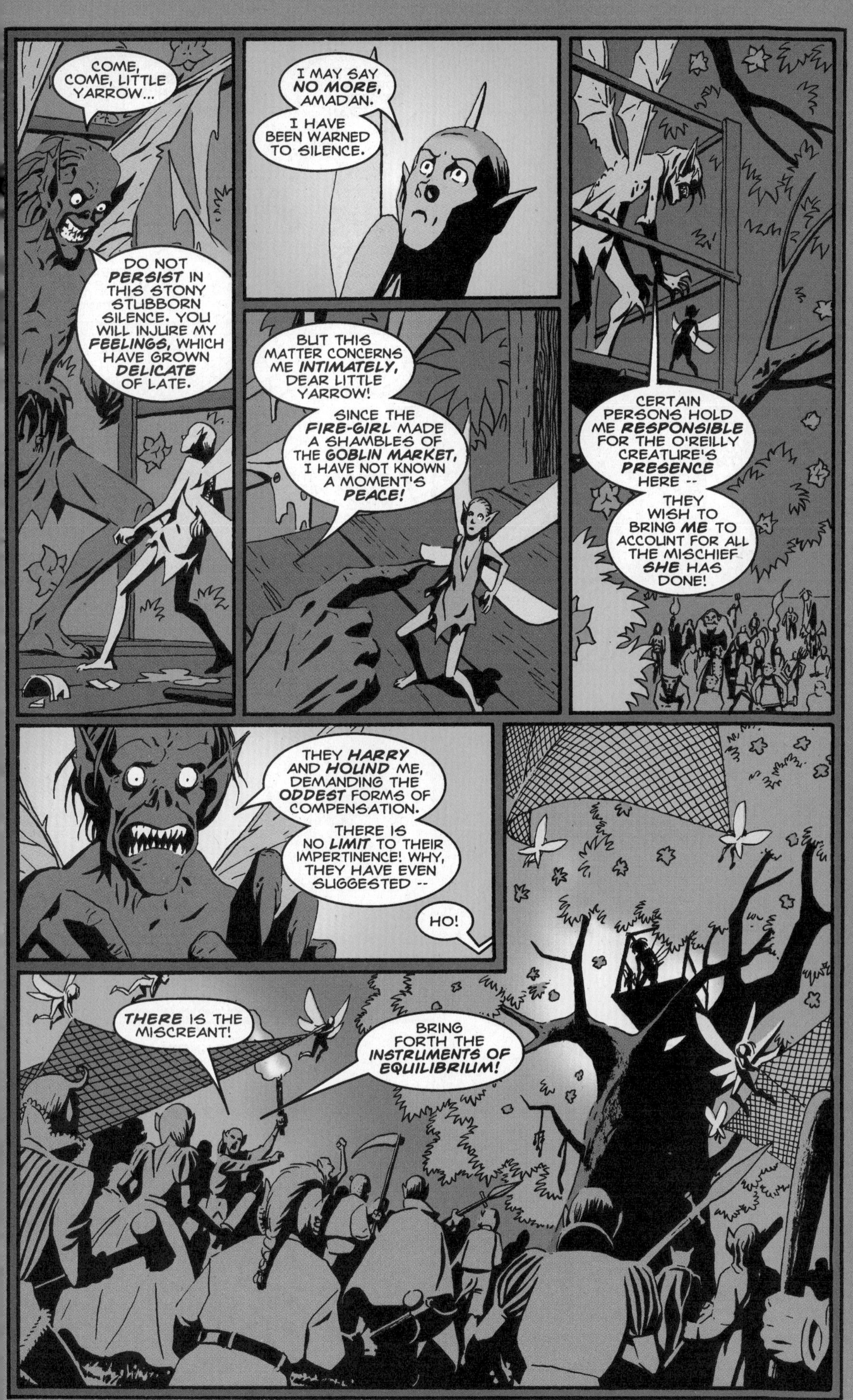
COME, COME, LITTLE YARROW...
DO NOT PERSIST IN THIS STONY STUBBORN SILENCE. YOU WILL INJURE MY FEELINGS, WHICH HAVE GROWN DELICATE OF LATE.
I MAY SAY NO MORE, AMADAN.
I HAVE BEEN WARNED TO SILENCE.
BUT THIS MATTER CONCERNS ME INTIMATELY, DEAR LITTLE YARROW!
SINCE THE FIRE-GIRL MADE A SHAMBLES OF THE GOBLIN MARKET, I HAVE NOT KNOWN A MOMENT'S PEACE!
CERTAIN PERSONS HOLD ME RESPONSIBLE FOR THE O'REILLY CREATURE'S PRESENCE HERE --
THEY WISH TO BRING ME TO ACCOUNT FOR ALL THE MISCHIEF SHE HAS DONE!
THEY HARRY AND HOUND ME, DEMANDING THE ODDEST FORMS OF COMPENSATION.
THERE IS NO LIMIT TO THEIR IMPERTINENCE! WHY, THEY HAVE EVEN SUGGESTED --
HO!
THERE IS THE MISCREANT!
BRING FORTH THE INSTRUMENTS OF EQUILIBRIUM!

Ulp
YOU ARE A FORTUNATE INDIVIDUAL, AMADAN.
A UNIQUE EXPERIENCE CLEARLY AWAITS YOU.
WHAT PURPOSE CAN THOSE REMARKABLY SERRATED INSTRUMENTS SERVE, I WONDER?
I HAVE NEVER SEEN THE LIKE.
SKY-SIEVES --
THEY BRING SKY-SIEVES!
HOW SHALL I ESCAPE THE LOUTS WITH WINGS SNARED IN TANGLE-WEB?
I KNOW A WAY.

THE HALL OF REFLECTIONS.

YARROW, DEAR KIND YARROW -- HOW MAY I ELUDE THEM?
HASTE IS OF THE ESSENCE! DESCRIBE THIS PLAN TO ME!
NO, NO...
I OUGHT NOT TO HAVE SPOKEN.
I AM NO PLANNER OF PLANS. THIS IS PLAIN TO ME, NOW.
THESE VILLAINS MEAN TO INFLICT ATROCIOUS PANGS UPON MY PERSON! WOULD YOU HAVE THEM SUCCEED?
DISCLOSE YOUR PLAN AT ONCE, CLEVER YARROW! HAVE DONE WITH THIS UNSEEMLY SELF-DEPRECATION!
BUT YOU WILL TAKE OFFENSE IF I SPEAK, AND BEHAVE UNCOUTHLY TOWARD ME!
YOU ARE A PROUD SPIRIT, AMADAN. YOU WOULD FIND MY PLAN DEMEANING.
I SWEAR BY MY NAME THAT I SHALL HOLD YOU BLAMELESS, DEAR YARROW, HOWEVER UNDIGNIFIED YOUR PLAN MAY BE!
ONLY SPEAK! AND I SHALL FOLLOW YOUR INSTRUCTIONS, NEVER HESITATING FOR AN INSTANT!
SO BE IT...
FOOL!

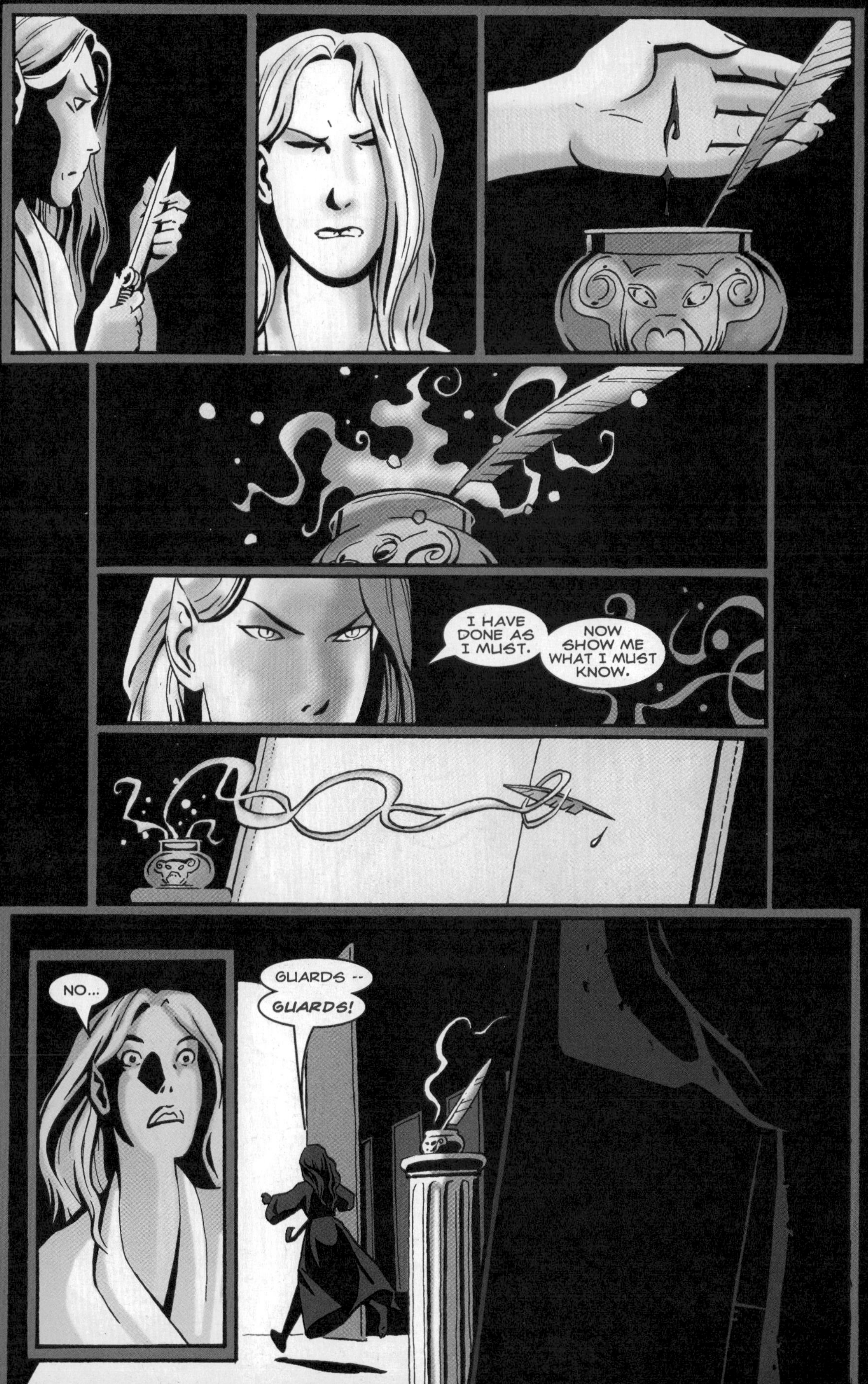

I HAVE DONE AS I MUST.
NOW SHOW ME WHAT I MUST KNOW.

NO...
GUARDS --
GUARDS!

IT DOESN'T MATTER WHAT THE STUPID VOICES SAY.
I DON'T LIKE TALKING ABOUT THAT STUFF, ALL RIGHT?

TALKING ABOUT IT ONLY MAKES IT WORSE.

BUT HOW CAN THE SHARING OF YOUR TROUBLES OPPRESS YOU?
I WISH TO HELP YOU, MOLLY. WILL YOU NOT CONFIDE IN ME?
I DON'T NEED ANY HELP.
I KNOW EXACTLY WHAT I NEED TO DO.

I NEED TO TAKE MY MEDICINE.
ONLY I HAVEN'T GOT ANY.

UNLESS --
Oh, CHRIST, SHE MIGHT HAVE.
SOMETIMES SHE KNOWS THE STRANGEST THINGS...

COME ON.
WE'VE GOT TO GO BACK TO THE TREEHOUSE. I LEFT MY SATCHEL THERE, I THINK --

YOUR SATCHEL?
THAT'S RIGHT, MY SATCHEL.

GRANNY FIONA PACKED IT FOR ME, JUST BEFORE I CAME HERE. AND SHE KNOWS WHAT'S GOING TO HAPPEN BEFORE IT HAPPENS.

THERE'S A LITTLE POCKET IN THE SATCHEL THAT I CAN NEVER GET UNSNAPPED. GRANNY'S ALWAYS TEASING ME ABOUT IT.
SHE SAYS MY FINGERS AREN'T OLD ENOUGH TO WORK IT.

I DON'T KNOW WHAT'S IN IT NOW... IF THERE'S ANYTHING IN IT.
BUT IF GRANNY KNEW I'D WIND UP GETTING STUCK HERE AND GOING LOOPY, THEN MAYBE --

MOLLY.
WHAT?

YOU HEAR VOICES--

AND YOU SEE THINGS, TOO, DO YOU?
DO YOU?
WHAT ARE YOU SEEING NOW?
ARE YOU SEEING NOW?

GET **STUFFED**. I DON'T HAVE ***TIME*** FOR THIS.
I'M GOING TO GET MY ***SATCHEL***.

YOU CAN STAY HERE AND BE PSYCHOLOGICAL ***BY YOURSELF*** IF YOU WANT.

WHAT IF YOU ARE **NOT** SICK, MOLLY?
YOUR ***GRANDMOTHER*** HAS THE SIGHT, DOES SHE NOT?

WHAT IF ALL YOU HEAR AND SEE TRULY IS, SOMEHOW?
TRUST ME, IT CAN'T BE.
I KNOW IT CAN'T, BECAUSE I KNOW YOU.
THEN LOOK AT ME, MOLLY LOOK AT US, FEY GIRL --
TELL ME TELL US --
WHAT DO YOU WHO DO YOU SEE?
GET AWAY FROM ME!

IT IS AS THE BOOK FORETOLD, MY LORDS...
THE BLACK SHIP COMES OUT OF SEASON.
SOON, I FEAR, WE SHALL KNOW WHO CAPTAINS HER.

SEE?
WHERE THEY WALK, THE EARTH CRACKS AND BLEEDS AND CRIES.
THESE ARE NOT HELL'S EMISSARIES.
THESE ARE HELL'S LORDS.

CLAK
CLAK
CLAK

I CHARGE THEE, BY THE COMPACT: SPEAK WITHOUT GUILE.
WHAT IS YOUR ERRAND HERE? IT IS NOT THE YEAR OF THE TEIND...

THE COMPACT?
HAHAHAA!

BETWEEN HELL AND THE SUMMERLAND THERE IS NO COMPACT, LADY.
THE COMPACT HAS BEEN BROKEN.
SPLINTERED AS MY EYES!

ONE OF THOSE WHOSE LIFE WAS TITHED TO US HAS SHIRKED HIS OBLIGATION.
ESCAPED FROM HELL AND FLED, LADY...

AND RETURNED HERE...
AS YOU KNOW.

AND NOT ALONE, OH NO.

Young Timothy Hunter, destined to become the world's greatest mage, left England hoping to escape the sorcerous and personal woes that plagued him there. But now his ex-girlfriend Molly is blazing through Faerie, suffering the fiery effects of Queen Titania's curse, and the torments of Titania's son Taik. Meanwhile, Tim remains trapped on a small island off of Faerie, just as hell's lords have arrived on Faerie's shores.

THE ONLY TIME I HAVE IS THE TIME I MAKE FOR MYSELF.
NO ONE ELSE HAS TO DO THAT.
OTHER PEOPLE HAVE TIME WITHOUT MAKING IT.
THEY ARE JUST BECAUSE THEY ARE.
THEIR FACES ARE BORN ON THEM, NOT CARVED AND EATEN INTO PLACE.
THEIR FACES STAY ALIVE AND CHANGE ALL BY THEMSELVES.
I DON'T HAVE ANYTHING UNLESS I MAKE IT, NOW...
NOW THAT KING HUON IS DEAD.
NO TIME. NO SHAPE. NO FACE.
NO SELF.
BUT SOMEDAY I WILL HAVE A FACE WHICH WILL BE A PERFECT PICTURE OF MY SOUL.
THEN I WILL HAVE A SELF AGAIN...
WITHOUT SCREAMING, WITHOUT DANCING...
WITHOUT CARVING OR EATING.
IT IS HARD TO FIND, THAT FACE.
MY SOUL CHANGES EVERY DAY.

ONCE I ATE A PIECE OF GLASS WHICH WAS BIGGER THAN I WAS.
IT DID NOT MAKE A GOOD FACE. I DID NOT WEAR IT FOR VERY LONG.

WHAT THE GLASS AND I FELT LIKE THEN IS WHAT IT FEELS LIKE TO BE ME ALWAYS.

SHARP AND CLEAR AND SPLINTERING.
TOO MUCH TO FIT INSIDE MYSELF.

I AM HUON.
HUON THE BLANK. HUON OF SEEMINGS.
I CAN DO THINGS THAT NO ONE ELSE CAN DO.

BECAUSE I AM ALWAYS WHAT I APPEAR TO BE.

NO MORE...

NO LESS.

Elsewhere.
You never know where you'll wind up, falling out of trees.
I think this is Faerie, but who knows?
I don't even know how I got here.

You can't always tell where you are.
You can be somewhere you think you've been a thousand times before, and still be totally lost.

They're a lot like people, places are.

They change...

But they're not really likely to warn you first...

Or tell you how they've changed...
Or why.

SKURCH

NOT AGAIN --
I've really had about enough of this.
SHRAK

It doesn't seem to matter what I do...
Or what I undo, either.

Every time I try to leave that stupid island, I do something wrong...
And I wind up shipwrecked here.

So I go back.
I've got to, don't I?

To start over.
To build my raft again.

But it gives me such a weird sad feeling, undoing does...
Every time.

Like I've just thrown part of my life away.
Like a little piece of me has turned to stone.
Reasons to be Stone
Rites of Passage Part 10
Timothy Hunter and the Books of Magic created by Neil Gaiman and John Bolton
John Ney Rieber writer
Peter Snejbjerg artist
Richard Starkings & Comicraft/LA letters
Sherilyn van Valkenburgh colors
Neil Gaiman consultant
Julie Rottenberg editor

YOUR EARS HANG ALL ASKANCE, AND YOUR FUR RESEMBLES A THREADBARE RUG.

STILL, I KNOW YOU. YOU ARE DRU, FOR WHOSE SAKE THE LAMIA KERSIS PERISHED OF LONGING.

-SIGH-

SO I AM.

HOW DID YOU KNOW ME?

I SO SELDOM WALK ABROAD IN THIS, MY OWN TRUE SEEMING...

I CANNOT SAY.

MY INTUITION LEADS A CURIOUS SOLITARY LIFE, SOMEWHERE IN THE DEPTHS OF MY BELLY.

IT IS FURTIVE AS A TWABBLE-CAT, AND SELDOM INFORMS ME OF ITS REASONS FOR SUPPOSING THIS OR THAT.

BUT IT IS CURIOUS, IS IT NOT, THAT WE SHOULD BOTH CHOOSE TO GO GUISELESS IN THE WORLD...
WHEN TRAGEDY HAS BEFALLEN US?

AYE... IT IS INDEED STRANGE.
I WONDER HOW MANY OF THE REST OF US WALK ABROAD AS OURSELVES TODAY?

IT IS DIFFICULT, VERY DIFFICULT, TO SAY... BUT I SEE MANY A FACE IN THE CROWD WHOSE EXPRESSIONS I CAN EXPLAIN NO OTHER WAY.

WHAT DID YOU LOSE IN THE BURNING?
EVERYTHING.
I WOULD ELUCIDATE, BUT TO SAY MORE WOULD TEAR MY HEART, AND TELL YOU LITTLE...
WHAT OF YOU?

I LOST MY HOME TO THE ACCURSED FIRE-WITCH.
SWEET FOXFIRE COVERT IS NO MORE.

I DID NOT KNOW THAT IT WAS MY HOME...
UNTIL IT WAS GONE.

DRU? YOU ARE A GOBLIN OF KEEN INTUITION. TELL ME -- DO YOU TRULY HOLD THE AMADAN ACCOUNTABLE FOR THE RUIN WHICH HAS OVERTAKEN US ALL?
NO.
NOR DOES ANY OTHER WHO MARCHES IN THIS COMPANY.

STILL, IT WILL EASE OUR HEARTS TO PLAY CAT'S-CRADLE WITH THE FOOL'S VISCERA, EH?

WE MUST DO SOMETHING TO STILL THE FEELING...
THE KNOWING WHAT WE HAVE LOST...

-snif-

DRAG THE TRAITOR FROM HIS SHELTER!
LET JUSTICE BE SERVED!

LET US SEE THE COLOR OF HIS BLOOD!
KILL THE FOOL!

FETCH THE INSTRUMENTS OF EQUILIBRIUM! THE TIME HAS COME!
TO THE TREE! TO THE TREE!
THE FOOL MUST ATONE FOR HIS CRIMES!
BUT WAIT --
WHO IS THIS WHO RISES FROM THE VILLAIN'S PLACE OF REFUGE?
SHE LAUGHS, SHE SHIMMERS, SHE SHINES --
HURRAH!
CAN THIS BE LITTLE YARROW, THE MEEKEST OF US ALL?
SHE HAS DEPRIVED THE AMADAN OF HIS HEAD!

HURRAH FOR ME!
I HAVE DONE WHAT NO FLITLING HAS EVER DONE!

I HAVE TRICKED THE AMADAN!
THE FOOL OF THE FORTHING IS A FOOL NO MORE, BUT A STONE --
AND A FALLEN STONE AND A BROKEN ONE, AT THAT.

Ohhh...
THE FOLK BELOW SEE ME.
THEY GAPE AND STARE AND POINT AT ME...

Ohh, I AM FRIGHTENED.
WHY MUST THEY LOOK AT ME? I AM NO ONE.
THEY MUST CEASE AT ONCE, OR I SHALL SURELY DIE --

WHAT SHALL I DO?
I CANNOT CHARM MYSELF FROM SIGHT WHILE FOLK ARE WATCHING. I --

WHAT IS TROUBLING THE SKY?
THE WIND HOWLS AND TWISTS, AND STINGS LIKE A FER-DE LANCE...

IT IS THE BLACK SHIP.

BUT WHY?
THIS IS NOT THE YEAR OR SEASON OF THE PAYMENT OF THE TEIND...

THE GREAT FOLK WAIT BEHIND CASTLE WALLS WHILE THE QUEEN GOES FORTH TO GREET THE DEMONS...
Ahhh, HOW COLD HER HEART MUST BE, TO FACE THE MASKS THEY WEAR WITH SUCH A SMILE!

SOMETHING MUST BE DONE. THE FOLK BELOW SUSPECT NOTHING...
BUT WHEN THE GREAT LORDS AND LADIES AND THE DEMONS MEET, IT IS ALWAYS THE FOLK OF HEDGE AND MEADOW WHO PAY THE PRICE...

BUT WHAT CAN I DO?
I AM A FLITLING.

AND I CANNOT EVEN *DISAPPEAR*.

WE AWAIT YOUR ANSWER, LADY.
WHAT SHALL IT BE?
WILL YOU RETURN YOUR SON TAIK TO OUR CARE --?
OUR TENDER CARE --
AND MAKE REPARATION FOR THE BREAKING OF THE COMPACT?
OR SHALL FIRE AND IRON RESTORE TO HELL'S POSSESSION THE LAND WHICH LUCIFER ONCE CEDED YOU?
BE PROUD, LADY... PLEASE, BE COURAGEOUS!
SPIT IN OUR FACES. DEFY US.
THERE IS SO LITTLE REAL PLEASURE TO BE HAD IN BUTCHERING THE DAMNED, NOWADAYS.
SO FEW OF THEM TRULY STRUGGLE.

ALAS...
BETWEEN YOUR FOLK AND MINE THERE SHALL BE NO BATTLE.
WHERE IS YOUR LEGENDARY SUBTLETY, TITANIA?
IT IS A SHABBY LITTLE LIE YOU OFFER US. AND WE ARE CONNOISSEURS OF UNTRUTH.
CLEARLY OUR VISIT COMES AS NO SURPRISE TO YOU, LITTLE QUEEN.
I SEE BOWMEN ON THE BATTLEMENTS OF YOUR CASTLE. I SENSE WAR-MAGIC SEETHING THERE.
AND I TASTE FEAR, LITTLE QUEEN. YOUR FEAR.
AND IT IS HOURS STALE.

IT IS TRUE THAT I ANTICIPATED YOUR ARRIVAL, MY LORDS. THE BOOK OF A SINGLE PAGE FORETOLD IT.
BUT THESE PREPARATIONS ARE NOT FOR THE LIKES OF YOU.
I DO NOT KNOW WHY HE SHOULD MANIFEST HIMSELF HERE...
BUT IF THE BOOK IS TO BE BELIEVED?
THE LEVELLER COMES TO THIS PLACE --
IF HE IS NOT HERE ALREADY.

CHIK
SLISHK
CHAK
CHAK
CHIK
SLISHK
CHAK
CHAK
WHITHER ARE YOU BOUND IN SUCH *HASTE*, MY LORDS?
FASTER, FASTER--
DO YOU WISH TO MEET THE LEVELLER?
LORDS, THE SHIP WILL NOT SAIL.

"WHAT DO YOU SEE?"
WHAT DO YOU SEE, MOLLY MY QUEEN?
I CAN'T.
Oh GOD, Oh GOD, I CAN'T SEE ANYTHING --
THERE'S NOTHING BUT FIRE...
AND GOD, IT'S IN MY EYES AND IT HURTS --
TAIK --
TAIK?
ARE YOU STILL HERE?

YOU TRULY CANNOT SEE ME?

Oh, WHAT HAVE YOU DONE, MOLLY?
THE BLAZE OF YOUR ANGER HAS BURNT YOUR SIGHT AWAY, POOR LAMB...
DID YOUR MOTHER NEVER WARN YOU NOT TO PLAY WITH FIRE?

YOU WILL BE NEEDING SOMEONE TO TAKE CARE OF YOU NOW, I SUPPOSE.
WHAT I NEED IS A BIG STICK, AND SOMEONE TO TELL ME WHERE YOU ARE.

WHY ARE YOU TALKING TO ME LIKE THIS?
I THOUGHT YOU CARED FOR ME, FOR GOD'S SAKE --
CHRIST, YOU ASKED ME TO MARRY YOU.

PART OF ME DOES CARE FOR YOU, MOLLY.
PART OF ME WOULD DIE FOR YOU IF NEED BE, AND GLADLY.

BUT IT IS A SMALL PART OF ME, FEY GIRL --
AND I AM EATING IT NOW, BITE BY BITE, AND IT IS SCREAMING.

SCREAMING YOUR NAME, INCIDENTALLY. AND NOT ITS OWN...
OR MINE, AS THE SOULS AND BODIES IN MY KEEPING TEND TO SCREAM, MORE OFTEN, THAN NOT.
IF YOU CLOSE YOUR POOR SEARED EYES, YOU SHOULD BE ABLE TO SEE ME AS I AM.
YOU REALLY OUGHT TO, MY DARLING --BEFORE I GROW TOO MUCH DARKER AND VASTER.
IT WOULD, I AM SURE, ENHANCE YOUR APPRECIATION OF THE LIFE YOU MIGHT-- WELL, PERHAPS NOT ENJOY,-- BUT EXPERIENCE AS ONE OF MY QUEENS.
DON'T HOLD YOUR --
Oh, I TAKE IT BACK.
DO HOLD YOUR BREATH.
FUMF

I HAVE A CONFESSION TO MAKE, MOLLY DARLING.
YOU DO NOT INTEREST ME. YOUR POWER DOES.

MY ARMY AWAITS ME, OUTSIDE THE PALACE OF THE MOTHER OF THIS FLESH I WEAR.
SHE IS YOUR ENEMY, IS GOOD QUEEN TITANIA...
YOU HATE HER, DO YOU NOT?

WOULDN'T YOU LOVE TO DO TO HER WHAT YOU DID TO THIS FOREST?
GET STUFFED.

Tsk. I BEHAVE QUITE BADLY WHEN I AM DISAPPOINTED, MOLLY DARLING.
ARE YOU SURE THAT YOU WOULDN'T PREFER A NICE WARM AFTERNOON OF FIRE-RAISING TO BEING STRANGLED AND TOSSED INTO A DITCH?

COME ON, BIG MOUTH --
LET'S JUST SEE WHO WINDS UP IN THE DITCH.

DO NOT BE FRIGHTENED, MOLLY...
THE BEAST SHALL NOT HARM YOU.

I WILL BE YOUR EYES.

Ehem

YOU ARE TRESPASSING.
I AM?

TRESPASSING IN MY DOMAIN.
THIS IS A DOMAIN?

EVERY BLUR AND QUIVER OF IT.
SORRY... I DIDN'T REALIZE.
I THOUGHT IT WAS JUST A FOG FROM HELL.

Oh, NO... NO NO NO, BOY.
NO.

THERE IS NO FOG IN HELL HALF SO MADDENING AS MY HOME.

FOR IN THE HOUSE WHICH LUCIFER BUILT IS A PLACE OF CERTAINTY...

IN ONE RESPECT, AT LEAST:
THE DAMNED KNOW THAT THEY ARE DAMNED.

BUT IN THE HOUSE THAT HUON BUILT?

WE CAN BE SURE OF NOTHING.

PREPARE YOURSELF.
WE MUST GO.

GO?

WE HAVE NO CHOICE.

WE NEVER DO, WE OPENERS AND LEVELLERS AND OTHERS AND THE LIKE.
WE DO WHAT WE MUST.
SNAP
HEY --
MY KEY --

YOUR WHAT?
HOW MANY TIMES HAVE YOU MISTAKEN THIS FOR A KEY, BOY?

THERE ARE NO KEYS FOR FREAKS LIKE YOU AND ME.
ONLY PRISONS.

Young Timothy Hunter, destined to become the world's greatest mage, left England hoping to escape the sorcerous and personal woes that plagued him there. But now his ex-girlfriend Molly is blazing through Faerie, suffering the fiery effects of Queen Titania's curse, and blinded by the torments of Titania's son Taik. While Faerie defends itself against the arrival of hell's lords, Tim discovers the many different faces of Huon the small.

LOCKED IN

Timothy Hunter & The Books of Magic created by Neil Gaiman & John Bolton.

John Ney Rieber WRITER
Peter Snejbjerg ARTIST
Sherilyn van Valkenburgh COLORIST
Richard Starkings & Comicraft/LA LETTERING
Jamison Services SEPARATIONS
Neil Gaiman CONSULTANT
Julie Rottenberg EDITOR

WHETHER YOU WISH TO OR NOT?

Oh, STOP TWISTING YOUR MOUTH LIKE THAT.
YOU ARE MUCH TOO YOUNG TO HAVE SEEN FOR YOURSELF THE CHILDISH DREAMS AND DREADS WHICH BIND YOU TO THIS PLACE.

I HAD TO MAKE THOUSANDS AND THOUSANDS OF EYES FOR MYSELF BEFORE I LEARNED HOW TO NOTICE OBVIOUS THINGS LIKE THAT.
YOU DON'T SAY.
BUT I DO. Ahhh...

CAN YOU TASTE IT? UNCERTAINTY SEETHES AND FERMENTS IN THE AIR...
IT IS TIME FOR US TO BEGIN THE LEVELLING.
WHAT?

WHEN THE DISPARITY BETWEEN THE SUBSTANCE OF A WORLD AND ITS APPEARANCE BECOMES TOO EXTREME, THESE ASPECTS OF ITS BEING CAN NO LONGER COEXIST.

THE MASKS WHICH THE SHAPERS OF THIS REALM NOW WEAR MUST EITHER BE DISCARDED, OR BECOME IN TRUTH THEIR FACES.

THIS WORLD MUST SWIFTLY DECIDE WHAT IT OUGHT TO BE...
OR IT WILL SOON CEASE TO BE.

AND HOW IS A WORLD SUPPOSED TO DECIDE WHAT IT OUGHT TO BE, IF YOU DON'T MIND MY ASKNG?
IT CAN'T EXACTLY ASK MARJ PROOPS, CAN IT?
SHE'S DEAD.
YOU ARE ABSOLUTELY RIGHT.
WORLDS DO NOT RECEIVE THEIR FACES FROM THE DEAD.
THAT IS WHY WE ARE HERE.

ELSEWHERE.

CAPTAIN?

YOU MUST NOT LINGER HERE, LADY. THE HELL-FOLK BELOW GROW SURLY.

THEIR FEAR OF THE LEVELLER'S ADVENT EXCEEDS EVEN OUR OWN.

WHERE HAS THE MOB GONE?

AMADAN-- WHAT HAS HAPPENED HERE?

SPEAK!

I AM STONE.
STILL, I AM YOUR KING, AND YOU WILL ANSWER ME.
SPEAK!

FOLK FROM EVERY CORNER OF THE LAND SOUGHT TO PUNISH ME FOR BRINGING THE FIRE-WITCH HERE TO BURN THEIR HOMES.
TO ESCAPE THEIR SKY-SNARES AND PIG-STICKERS, I SWORE A GREAT OATH TO FOLLOW A FLITLING'S COUNSEL.

HER EYES WERE MEEK AND MILD AS WATERED MILK! HOW COULD I GUESS SHE MEANT ME HARM?
STILL, SHE BADE ME MAKE A STATUE OF MYSELF, AND LAUGHED WHEN I TOPPLED FROM THE TREEHOUSE!

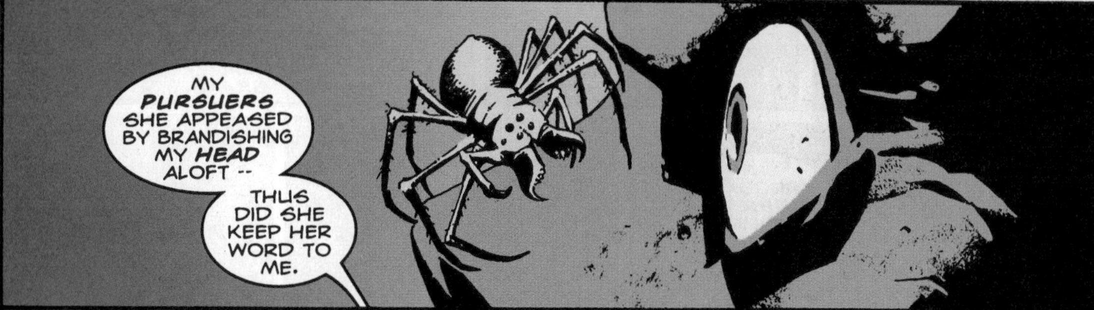
MY PURSUERS SHE APPEASED BY BRANDISHING MY HEAD ALOFT --
THUS DID SHE KEEP HER WORD TO ME.

I HAVE SWORN TO BEAR HER NO ILL-WILL, ELSE I SHOULD CURSE HER BONES TO KRINK.
BUT SHE HAS TRICKED ME ALL TOO WELL.

I AM THE FOOL OF THE FORTHING NO LONGER, MAJESTY.
INSIPID LITTLE YARROW IS THE GREAT FOOL OF FAERIE, NOW.

AND WHAT OF THE FOLK WHO HUNTED YOU?
WHAT HAS BECOME OF THEM?
THE FLITLING HURLED MY HEAD INTO THEIR MIDST, TO GAIN THEIR ATTENTION --

THEN SHE SPOKE TO THE LOUTS OF THEIR VANISHED HOMES...
...UNTIL ALL WHO HAD EYES WEPT LIKE CHANGELINGS.

I DID NOT HEAR HER PARTING REMARKS, FOR A TROLL THEN BOOTED MY HEAD INTO THIS FERN-BRAKE.

AN ARROGANT SPIDER HAS TROUBLED ME EVER SINCE, DEAR AUBERON.
PERHAPS YOU WOULD CRUSH THE MALEVOLENT LITTLE CLIMBER FOR ME?

WHY DO YOU HESITATE, GREAT KING?
JUSTICE DEMANDS THAT THIS CREATURE SHOULD PERISH!

HE IS INCORRIGIBLY VAIN AND VICIOUS!
AND HE POSTURES UNBEARABLY!

WHAT DO YOU KNOW OF THE TEIND?
IT'S NOT SOMETHING YOU SLEEP IN WHEN YOU GO CAMPING?
HARDLY.
THEN I'VE NEVER HEARD OF IT.
BUT YOU HAVE HEARD OF HELL?
HEARD OF IT? I'VE BEEN THERE. I KNOW HELL, ALL RIGHT.
I WONDER.
LOOK AROUND YOU. WHAT DO YOU SEE?
FAERIE.
YOU KNOW... THAT PLACE WHERE ALL THE FAIRIES LIVE.
AND HOW DOES IT APPEAR TO YOU?
WHAT, THE GREEN PARTS OR THE BURNING PARTS?
DO NOT MOCK YOUR VISION, CHILD OF EARTH. SPEAK FROM THE HEART.
TELL ME WHAT YOU SEE.
IT'S BEAUTIFUL.
SO BEAUTIFUL IT'S ALMOST SCARY.
THIS BEAUTY YOU SEE?
IT BELONGS TO HELL.

NEARBY.
SPEAK SOFTLY, MOLLY. LET YOUR LIPS MOVE ONLY SLIGHTLY.
THE BEAST MUST CONTINUE TO BELIEVE YOU ARE ALONE.

PERHAPS I WILL NOT STRANGLE YOU AFTER ALL, MY DARLING. PERHAPS I WILL BREAK YOUR NECK INSTEAD.
DO YOU HAVE A PREFERENCE?

WALK SLOWLY BACKWARDS, NOW...
THREE STEPS...
NO, FOUR.

YOU DANCE NIMBLY NOW, BLIND GIRL...
BUT HOW WILL YOU AVOID MY HANDS WHEN I AM SILENT?

THAT WAS BRAVELY DONE! NOW CIRCLE DEASIL --
DEASIL?
TO YOUR RIGHT.

IF YOU'VE GOT A FAN CLUB, I'M JOINING.
WHO ARE YOU?

IS IT NOT OBVIOUS? I AM YOUR FRIEND.
YARROW IS MY NAME.

WE CANNOT RUN FROM THE BEAST, IT IS CLEAR. WE MUST FIGHT.
HOW SHALL WE BEGIN?

IS HIS BODY STILL THE SAME?
IS HE STILL JUST A BOY?
YES.
ALL RIGHT...

IF I CAN CATCH HIS WRIST?
HE'LL NEVER PLAY THE PIANO AGAIN.

Hist!
THE BEAST CREEPS UP BEHIND US.
WHEN YOU HEAR ME CRY YOUR NAME, TURN TOWARD MY VOICE, AND STRETCH OUT BOTH YOUR HANDS.

I WILL GIVE YOU HIS WRIST TO GRASP AND TWIST, IF I HAVE THE STRENGTH.
ONLY REMEMBER, MOLLY, WHEN THE BEAST IS IN YOUR HANDS --

THERE IS MORE TO YOU THAN FIRE.

YEAH.
RIGHT.

THINGS OFTEN *ARE* BEFORE THEY HAVE A PLACE TO BE, OPENER.
AND SO IT WAS WITH THE *FAIR FOLK*.

"THE *ELDEST* WERE CONCEIVED OF THE DREAMING OF THE *EARTH*, AND THE DREAMING OF THE *NIGHT SKY* STRETCHED ABOVE HER.

"THE *YOUNGEST* WERE BORN OF THE DREAMING OF THE EARTH AND THE DREAMING OF HER MORTAL CHILDREN.

"AND *BETWEEN* THOSE GENERATIONS, Ahh...
"THE EARTH HAS TAKEN *MANY* A STRANGE LOVER IN HER DREAMS, AND TO *ALL* SHE HAS EMBRACED, SHE HAS BORNE *CHILDREN*."

STRANGE CHILDREN, EARTH-CHILD --

SOME EVEN STRANGER THAN YOU.

"BUT TO BE *BORN* IS TO BE CONFINED WITHIN ONE'S MOTHER *NO LONGER*.

"THE FAIR FOLK FOUND *NO PLACE* FOR THEMSELVES IN THE DREAMS *OR* THE FLESH OF THE EARTH.

"THE SKY WHOSE DREAMS HAD FATHERED THE *ELDEST* OF THE FAIR FOLK GAVE THEM NO WELCOME BUT *DISTANCE* AND *COLD*...

"THE *MORTALS* WHOSE FANTASIES OF DREAD AND DESIRE HAD SHAPED THE *YOUNGEST* MET THEM WITH BLADES OF *COLD IRON*...

"OR STRATAGEMS OF *LUST* AND *AVARICE*.

"UNTIL ONE CAME TO THE NINE *LORDS* WHO RULED THEM, AND SAID: YOU WHO ARE *HOMELESS* AND *WEARY* IN THIS WORLD --

"COME WITH ME, AND I SHALL GIVE YOU *REST*."

"THE STRANGER LED THE EIGHT LORDS UP A MOUNTAIN.
"ONE SWORE THAT THE REEK OF SEARED FLESH CLUNG TO CERTAIN OF THE STONES THEY PASSED THERE...
"AND THAT HE HEARD STIFLED GROANS AND PEALS OF LAUGHTER ECHOING UP THE WAY.
"BUT WHATEVER HIS COMPANIONS MAY HAVE SEEN OR HEARD, NOT A ONE OF THEM SO MUCH AS SLOWED THEIR STEPS.
"AFTER A TIME, HE FOLLOWED THEM UP THE MOUNTAINSIDE.
"HE DID NOT KNOW WHAT ELSE TO DO.
"'LOOK DOWN,' THE STRANGER SAID, WHEN ALL HAD GAINED THE MOUNTAIN'S SUMMIT.
"BELOW THEM, THE EIGHT LORDS OF THE SIDHE SAW...
"Ahh, THE SAME BEAUTY YOU NOW SEE, OPENER.
"'I AM THE KING OF A NATION OF EXILES LIKE YOURSELVES,' THE STRANGER SAID. 'AND THE SYMPATHY I FEEL FOR YOU IS AS OVER-WHELMING AS THE LOVE I BEAR THE EARTH, YOUR MOTHER.'
"'ALL THAT YOU SEE BELOW YOU WILL I GIVE TO YOU, IF YOU WILL ONLY PAY HOMAGE TO ME.
"'EVERY SEVEN YEARS, LET SEVEN OF THE FAIREST AND WISEST OF YOUR PEOPLE JOIN ME IN MY REALM, AND THIS LAND SHALL BE YOUR HOME...'"

"WITHOUT HESITATION, SEVEN OF THE LORDS OF THE SIDHE **ACCEPTED** THE STRANGER'S BARGAIN.

"THE EIGHTH **HESITATED** BEFORE GIVING HIS CONSENT.

"THE **SEVEN** LUCIFER THEN BORE BACK TO **HELL** WITH HIM.

"**HUON THE MIRTHLESS,** HIS **PEOPLE** CALLED HIM...

"BEFORE THE SECRET **GUILT** HE BORE **CONSUMED** HIM, AND **UNCERTAINTY** MERCIFULLY **ERASED HIM** FROM THEIR WORLD AND FROM THEIR **MEMORY.**"

THE PEOPLE OF FAERIE DO NOT KNOW WHAT IT IS THAT THEY BUY WITH THEIR LIVES.
THE SECRET OF THE TEIND HAS BEEN DISCLOSED ONLY TO MY HEIRS AND SUCCESSORS, THE KINGS AND QUEENS OF FAERIE --

AND YOU.

WHY?
WHY TELL ME ALL THIS STUFF NO ONE'S SUPPOSED TO KNOW?

YOU WILL UNDERSTAND SOON ENOUGH, CHILD OF EARTH.

COME.

WE HAVE WORK TO DO.

NOW, GIRL --
IT ENDS FOR YOU.

MAKE HASTE, QUEEN TITANIA!
BRAVE DEEDS ARE DONE IN EVERGREEN WOOD!

GOOD PRINCE TAIK HAS RETURNED FROM THE DREADFUL DEMON-LANDS!
HE HAS CAPTURED THE FIRE-WITCH, THE ENEMY OF US ALL!

TITANIA?
HERE?

MOLLY!
SEIZE HIM, NOW --

UHNN
Hah!
YOU ARE CLEVER, LITTLE ONES... BUT WEAK.

AS I HAVE SAID BEFORE --
THERE ARE NO WARRIORS IN FAERIE, NOW THAT AUBERON IS GONE.
NOW, MOLLY...
LISTEN CLOSELY.
I AM GOING TO TEAR THE WINGS FROM YOUR CHAMPION'S BACK.
NO, DEMON --
TORMENTOR AND DEFILER OF MY SON --
YOU SHALL NOT.

TITANIA!
RECALL THIS MIST, OR WE ANSWER WITH HELLFIRE.
THIS MIST IS NONE OF MY DOING, LORDS.
I HAD THOUGHT IT YOURS.

I HAVE TRIED TO WORK AGAINST IT --
BUT I CAN NEITHER DISPEL NOR CONTAIN IT.

WHAT CAN WE DO?

WE WILL NOT EVEN BE ABLE TO SEE THE LEVELLER WHEN HE COMES...

BROTHER?
SISTER?

SOMEONE.
ANYONE.
HELP ME.

FEEL THE WORLD DISSOLVING AROUND YOU.
KNOW THAT YOU ARE UTTERLY ALONE.
MASTERS?
BROTHERS?
ASK YOURSELF --
WHO CREEPS AND SCUTTLES THROUGH THE FOG TOWARD YOU?

CRY OUT --
KNOWING IN YOUR HEART THAT YOU WILL NOT BE HEARD OR ANSWERED.
GUARDS!
WHOSE ARE THE FOOTFALLS YOU HEAR BEHIND YOU?
WHY ARE YOU AFRAID TO TURN?

WHOSE RAGGED BREATHING ECHOES YOURS?
WHERE ARE YOU?

ALWAYS WITHIN YOUR REACH...
FOREVER OUT OF SIGHT...

WHO WAITS FOR YOU?

YARROW?
AUBERON?

WHERE DID EVERYONE GO?

I DON'T BELIEVE IT --
IT'S GONE.

HOW COULD YOU JUST ERASE IT ALL LIKE THAT?

PEOPLE LIVED HERE --
NONE OF THEM KNEW WHO THEY WERE, OR WHAT THEY WANTED.
THEY HAVE BEEN LIVING IN HELL.

NOW THEY KNOW THAT.
NEXT: The CONCLUSION!

Young Timothy Hunter, destined to become the world's greatest mage, left England hoping to escape the sorcerous and personal woes that plagued him there. But now Tim is back in Faerie, where his ex-girlfriend Molly has been cursed by Queen Titania and blinded by Titania's son, Taik. Meanwhile, the constantly-changing Huon reveals to Tim the true story of how Faerie came to be, just as a mysterious fog is descending upon all the Faerieland...

MY NAME IS MARY ROSE.
WHAT'S YOURS?
MARY... MARY ROSE.
WE HAVE THE SAME NAME?
NO.
WHY...
WHY DO YOU LOOK SO SAD?
I ONCE KNEW SOMEONE VERY LIKE YOU, MARY ROSE.
AND EVERY DAY OF MY LIFE, I WONDER WHAT KIND OF WOMAN SHE WOULD HAVE GROWN TO BE...
IF I HAD NOT... BETRAYED HER.

BUT I WILL BUILD US A HOUSE ALL OUR **OWN,** AND WE SHALL HAVE **TEA** AND **CAKES...**

ELSEWHERE.

WHAT DO YOU MEAN, NOTHING'S CHANGED?

FAERIE'S GONE AND SO ARE THE FAIRIES.

NONSENSE.

FAERIE HAS LOST NOTHING BUT ITS SHAPE, AT THIS POINT.

AND THE SAME IS TRUE OF ITS INHABITANTS.

ELSEWHERE.
WHERE ARE YOU?
WHERE ARE YOU, DEMON?

WHERE ARE YOU?

EVERY KING WHO HAS EVER REIGNED IN FAERIE HAS KNOWN WHY WE PAY THE TEIND TO HELL.
HAIL, AUBERON -- KING OF THE DAMNED.

OR DO WE WALK IN HELL, NOW?

THIS IS A PLACE OF PAIN REMEMBERED.
WE ARE PROOF ENOUGH OF THAT.
BUT CERTAIN SIGNS SUGGEST TO ME THAT THIS PAIN...
MAY BE OVERCOME.

WHAT DO YOU THINK, MY BOLD WARRIOR KING?
MUCH CAN CHANGE WHEN A TIME OF LEVELLING COMES.

CAN YOU FIND IN YOURSELF THE COURAGE TO MAKE YOUR KINGDOM WHAT IT COULD BE?

YOU WHO MUST BEG HELP OF MORTAL CHILDREN BECAUSE YOU DARE NOT RULE YOUR SUBJECTS YOURSELF?

YOU WHO MUST GUISE YOURSELF AS A LADY OF THE COURT TO BE FRIEND AND BEDMATE TO YOUR WIFE?

YOU WHO PERMITTED A NOBLE SON TO BURN AND SUFFER IN HELL IN YOUR STEAD?

WHAT SAY YOU, MY LORD COWARD?

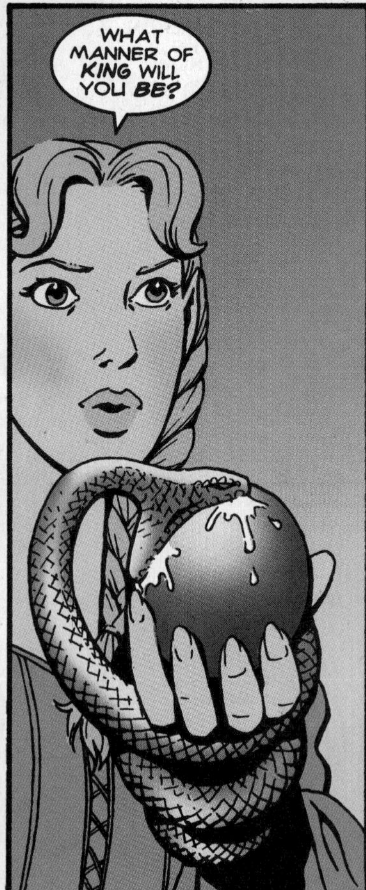
WHAT MANNER OF KING WILL YOU BE?

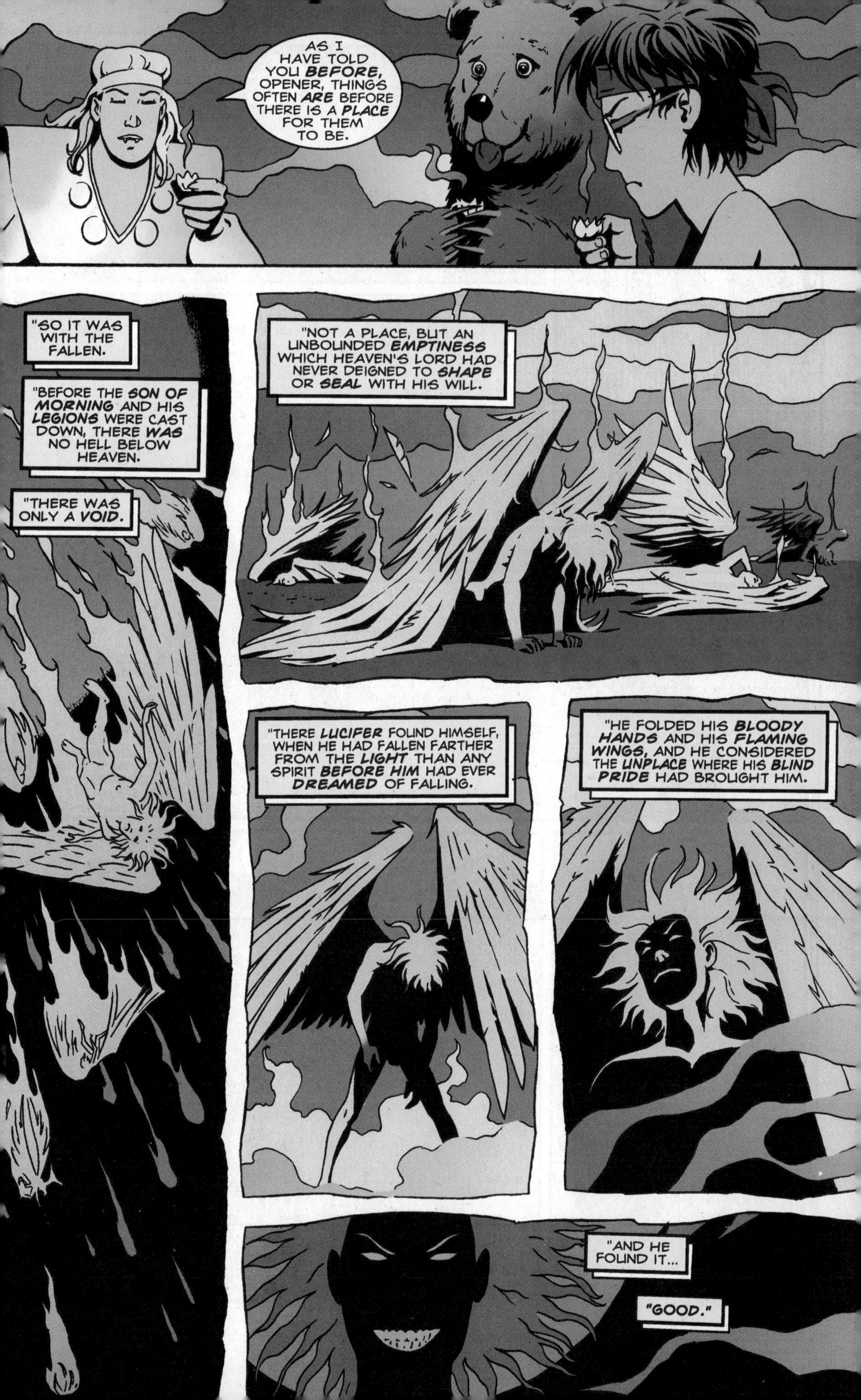

AS I HAVE TOLD YOU **BEFORE**, OPENER, THINGS OFTEN **ARE** BEFORE THERE IS A **PLACE** FOR THEM TO BE.

"SO IT WAS WITH THE FALLEN.

"BEFORE THE **SON OF MORNING** AND HIS **LEGIONS** WERE CAST DOWN, THERE **WAS** NO HELL BELOW HEAVEN.

"THERE WAS ONLY A **VOID**.

"NOT A PLACE, BUT AN UNBOUNDED **EMPTINESS** WHICH HEAVEN'S LORD HAD NEVER DEIGNED TO **SHAPE** OR **SEAL** WITH HIS WILL.

"THERE **LUCIFER** FOUND HIMSELF, WHEN HE HAD FALLEN FARTHER FROM THE **LIGHT** THAN ANY SPIRIT **BEFORE HIM** HAD EVER **DREAMED** OF FALLING.

YARROW!
AUBERON?

WHERE DID EVERYONE GO?

CHRIST, WHAT'S THE MATTER WITH YOU?
ARE YOU WHISPERING OR WHIMPERING?

THE VOICE SOUNDS BETTER ON ME, I THINK.
WHAT ARE YOU? ANOTHER FAIRY, OR ANOTHER DEMON?

ME, A DEMON?

YOU'RE THE ONE WHOSE HEAD IS ON FIRE.

WHERE DID EVERYONE GO?
HOW SHOULD I KNOW? I HAVE A HARD ENOUGH TIME KEEPING TRACK OF YOU.

I MEAN, CHRIST, LOOK AT YOU.
YOU'RE NOT YOU ANYMORE.
YOU'RE A BLOODY FAIRY TERRORIST.
YOU'VE LET YOURSELF GET SO ANGRY YOU'RE BLIND.

AND YOU CAME THIS CLOSE TO FALLING IN LOVE WITH A BOY YOU CAN ONLY TRUST WHEN HE'S A HORSE --

YOU KNOW, IF WE'D EVER HAD THAT STUPID TOURNAMENT OF FOOLS, THE AMADAN WOULD HAVE BEATEN ME.
HE WOULD HAVE TURNED ME TO STONE.

THAT USED TO FRIGHTEN ME.

BUT I THINK I'D LIKE TO BE A STONE, NOW.
I THINK I'D LIKE THAT VERY MUCH.

YOU KNOW YOU DON'T MEAN THAT.
YOU'D MAKE A TERRIBLE STONE.
YEAH. I WOULD.

DO YOU KNOW WHY YOU'RE SUCH A MESS?
IT'S NOT YOUR SITUATION.
YOU'VE NEVER HAD AN EASY LIFE.

BUT YOU'VE ALWAYS KNOWN WHO YOU COULD TRUST --
UNTIL TIM FLAKED OUT ON YOU.
AND GRANNY SENT YOU OFF TO BE ABDUCTED BY FAIRIES.

AND ONCE YOU WERE HERE IN FAERIE --
CHRIST, YOU CAN'T EVEN TRUST THE BLACKBERRIES HERE.

YOU'VE JUST GOT TO REMEMBER.
EVEN IF THERE'S NO ONE ELSE AROUND WHO YOU CAN COUNT ON...
YEAH... I KNOW...

LISTEN, WOULD YOU MIND BEING THE INDOMITABLE ONE FOR A WHILE?

I'M SHAGGED OUT.

LUCIFER SET THE FIRE OF HIS WILL UPON THE VOID, THEN...
-:-YAWN-:-
KLINK

"AND WHILE THE VOID RAGED WITH THE HEAT OF HIS FURY, HE SEALED IT WITH A SACRIFICE SUCH AS NONE BUT HE MIGHT MAKE...

"CONSECRATING THE SOUL OF THE BRIGHTEST OF ANGELS TO THE PURPOSE OF THE DARKEST OF DEMONS:
"OFFERING LUCIFER TO LUCIFER: HIMSELF TO HIMSELF.

"THE FALLEN TREMBLED.
"SPIRITS WHO HAD DARED CONTEND AGAINST THE ARCHANGELS MICHAEL AND GABRIEL...
"SPIRITS WHO HAD NOT FEARED TO FACE ARAQUEL THE DEATH-BRINGER IN BATTLE...

"EVEN THEY CRIED OUT, AND HID THEIR EYES FROM THE SIGHT.

"AND WHEN HE SAW THAT NO EYES IN HELL BUT HIS REMAINED OPEN, LUCIFER SPREAD WIDE HIS WINGS...
"AND THE LIGHT HE HAD BEEN CAST THE SHADOW HE HAD BECOME INTO THE VOID."

ABBADON.

GOOD DAY, PRINCE.
LOVELY WEATHER WE'RE HAVING, ISN'T IT?

WHAT WILL BECOME OF YOUR SOUL WHEN YOU DIE?
DO YOU KNOW?
NO, MY DARLING...
NOR SHALL I EVER.

Ahh, VERY NICE...
SO WE ARE TO PLAY AT BLADES AND BLOOD IN THE HOUSE OF DUST?
YOU ALWAYS WERE SENTIMENTAL.
DO YOU MISS THE DEAR OLD PLACE?

THERE IS NOWHERE I WOULD RATHER SEE YOU DIE.

HERE YOU TORMENTED ME AND TAINTED ME UNTIL I NO LONGER KNEW MYSELF --
UNTIL YOU COULD HIDE IN ME, LIKE A MAGGOT IN A PIECE OF MEAT --

AND I COULD NOT EVEN FEEL YOU THERE.

IF ONLY MOLLY HAD SENSED THE *TAINT* IN ME, AS *MOTHER* DID...
IF ONLY I HAD BEEN WISE ENOUGH TO *REMAIN* A HORSE FOREVER...

STILL, YOUR BLACK SHIP OF *TREACHERY* NEED NEVER HAVE SET SAIL.
YOU WILL *NEVER* RULE IN FAERIE.

THIS IS *MY* HELL --

AAAH--
NOT YOURS.

AND YOU... ARE *NOTHING*...

HERE.

AND HELL **SHAPED ITSELF** TO LUCIFER'S DESIRE...

"AND **SHROUDED** ITSELF, AS WAS HIS WILL, IN **DARKNESS**...

"**HIS** DARKNESS.

"AND FROM THAT DAY TO **THIS,** HELL'S TRUE SHAPE HAS BEEN **HIDDEN**...

"SAVE FROM THE EYES OF HIM WHOSE PRIDE AND POWER **SHAPED** IT.

"ONLY HE WHO **BUILDS** A HOUSE TRULY KNOWS IT."

WHY DO YOU WEAR SUCH A LONG FACE, SISTER?
YOU ARE FINALLY ALONE, AS YOU HAVE LONGED TO BE.

NO ONE WILL EVER FIND YOU HERE.

THE GREAT FOLK WILL NOT FRIGHTEN YOU WITH THEIR COLD LOOKS AND SHARP GLANCES.
NO DANGER WILL EVER THREATEN YOU.
AT LONG LAST, YOU ARE SAFE.

WILL I THEN THINK BRAVE, SOLITARY THOUGHTS, AS MOLLY DOES?
WILL I AT LAST BE ABLE TO SING AS SHE DOES?
HENCEFORTH YOU MAY DO JUST AS YOU PLEASE.
ARE YOU NOT ALONE?

YES...
BUT WHY MUST I BE ALONE TO FIND MY COURAGE AND MY VOICE?

MOLLY WAS NOT BRAVE BECAUSE SHE WAS SHELTERED FROM HARM.

SHE DID NOT SING BECAUSE HER LIFE WAS FREE OF TOIL AND TROUBLE.

FROM THE MOMENT SHE ENTERED FAERIE, SHE WAS DOOMED TO STRUGGLE... AND SHE KNEW THIS.

AND STILL SHE COULD SING.

CHUK

I MUST DO THE SAME.

I CANNOT REMAIN HERE.

I AM THE FOOL OF THE FORTHING, NOW.

I HAVE MUCH TO DO.

IN MY WORLD.

SO EVERYONE'S STILL HERE?
THEY ARE ALL AT LEAST POTENTIALLY SHAPERS OF THIS PLACE.
WHERE ELSE WOULD THEY BE?
AND THEY'RE ALL BY THEMSELVES...
LIKE I WAS, WHEN I WAS IN HELL...
NOT QUITE.
IT IS NO LONGER THE NATURE OF THIS PLACE TO ENTRAP SOULS.
STILL, THEY ARE ALONE WITH THEMSELVES.
I DOUBT THAT THEY ARE ENJOYING THE EXPERIENCE.
BUT THEY MUST DECIDE WHO THEY ARE SOMEHOW.
AND AT LEAST ONE OF THEM MUST CARE ENOUGH ABOUT THIS POOR, TATTERED WORLD TO DECIDE WHAT IT OUGHT TO BE, OR --
SHIT.
THIS IS MOLLY'S THERMOS FLASK.
YOU LISTEN TO ME.
SHE'S OUT THERE SOMEWHERE.
CALM YOURSELF, OPENER!
LISTEN TO ME --
LISTEN TO YOU?
YOU'RE SUCH A... A GONK THAT YOU DON'T EVEN HAVE A FACE.

ALL THIS FINDING-YOURSELF-BY-YOURSELF STUFF IS RIDICULOUS.
YOU CAN **LOSE YOUR MIND** ALL BY YOURSELF, BUT THAT'S ABOUT **ALL** THAT YOU CAN DO.
YOU FIGURE OUT WHO YOU ARE BY **BEING** WITH PEOPLE, NOT BY WALKING AROUND WRAPPED IN SOME BLOODY **FOG.**
GOD --
WHAT AM I TALKING TO **YOU** FOR?
I'M THE ONE WHO'S SUPPOSED TO BE THE **OPENER.**
I SUPPOSE IT'S TIME I ACTUALLY OPENED SOMETHING.
COME ON --
EVERYONE **OUT.**
STOP.

YOU ARE AS GENEROUS AS YOU ARE SIMPLE-MINDED, OPENER --
BUT YOU NEED NOT EXERT YOURSELF.
THIS WORLD HAS BEEN REBORN WITHOUT A MIDWIFE.
YOU MAY RETURN HOME NOW.
WAIT --
THE LEVELLER HAS DONE HER WORK.

HAIL, YARROW!
ALL OF FAERIE IS IN YOUR *DEBT*, LEVELLER...
THE REALM IS NOW WHAT IT *SHOULD* HAVE BEEN FROM THE BEGINNING.

REWARD YOUR FOOL *WELL*, AUBERON.
BECAUSE OF HER, FAERIE *ENDURES*...
AND IS *NO LONGER* BOUND TO PAY THE TEIND TO HELL.

YOUR *SON*, TOO, HAS BEEN RETURNED TO YOU.
HE WEARS THE SHAPE OF A *BEAST*, BUT HIS SOUL HAS BEEN CLEANSED OF *HELL-TAINT*.
MY LORD --
CAN THIS *BE*?

Oh, DON'T LOOK SO *WORRIED*.
YOU'LL BE *FINE*.
THAT MOB ISN'T *BRIGHT* ENOUGH TO MAKE YOU *QUEEN*.

WE ARE IN YOUR *DEBT*, YARROW.
WHAT IS YOUR *DESIRE*?

DO NOT ASK ME WHAT *I* WISH, MY KING.
YOU OWE ME *NOTHING*.
IT IS *MOLLY* YOU SHOULD THANK.

THE FIRE-WITCH?
SHE IS THE ONE WHO BURNED OUR HOMES!

QUEEN TITANIA BEARS THE BLAME FOR THAT, WHATEVER SHE MAY SAY --
BUT THIS IS BESIDE THE POINT.

I SEE NO TRACES OF THE BURNING ANYWHERE ON THE LAND.
AND I ASK YOU --

HOW MANY OF YOU WILL TREASURE THE HOMES YOU RETURN TO, NOW...
ONLY BECAUSE YOU HAVE LOST THEM?

MOLLY O'REILLY...

YOU KNOW WHAT I WANT.

I WANT TO GO HOME...
WITHOUT CRUMBLING INTO DUST, PREFERABLY.
I WANT TO SEE TIM.
I CANNOT RESTORE YOUR MORTALITY, MY CHILD.
BUT THIS MUCH I CAN DO:
YOU SHALL WALK UPON THE EARTH WITHOUT TOUCHING IT, AND SO COME TO NO HARM.
YOU SHALL HAVE FAIRY FOOD TO EAT WHEN YOU HUNGER FOR IT, AND SO BE SPARED THE WASTING SICKNESS.
FAREWELL, CHILD.
FORGIVE ME.

HEAR ME!

TODAY WE OWE OUR LIVES TO A CHILD OF EARTH --
A MORTAL AND A STRANGER.

NOW WE MUST ALL LIVE OUR LIVES...

LEST WE LOSE THEM AGAIN.

NOW --
TO YOUR HOMES, ALL OF YOU.

MY LADY AND MY HEIR AND I HAVE LIVES OF OUR OWN TO BEGIN.

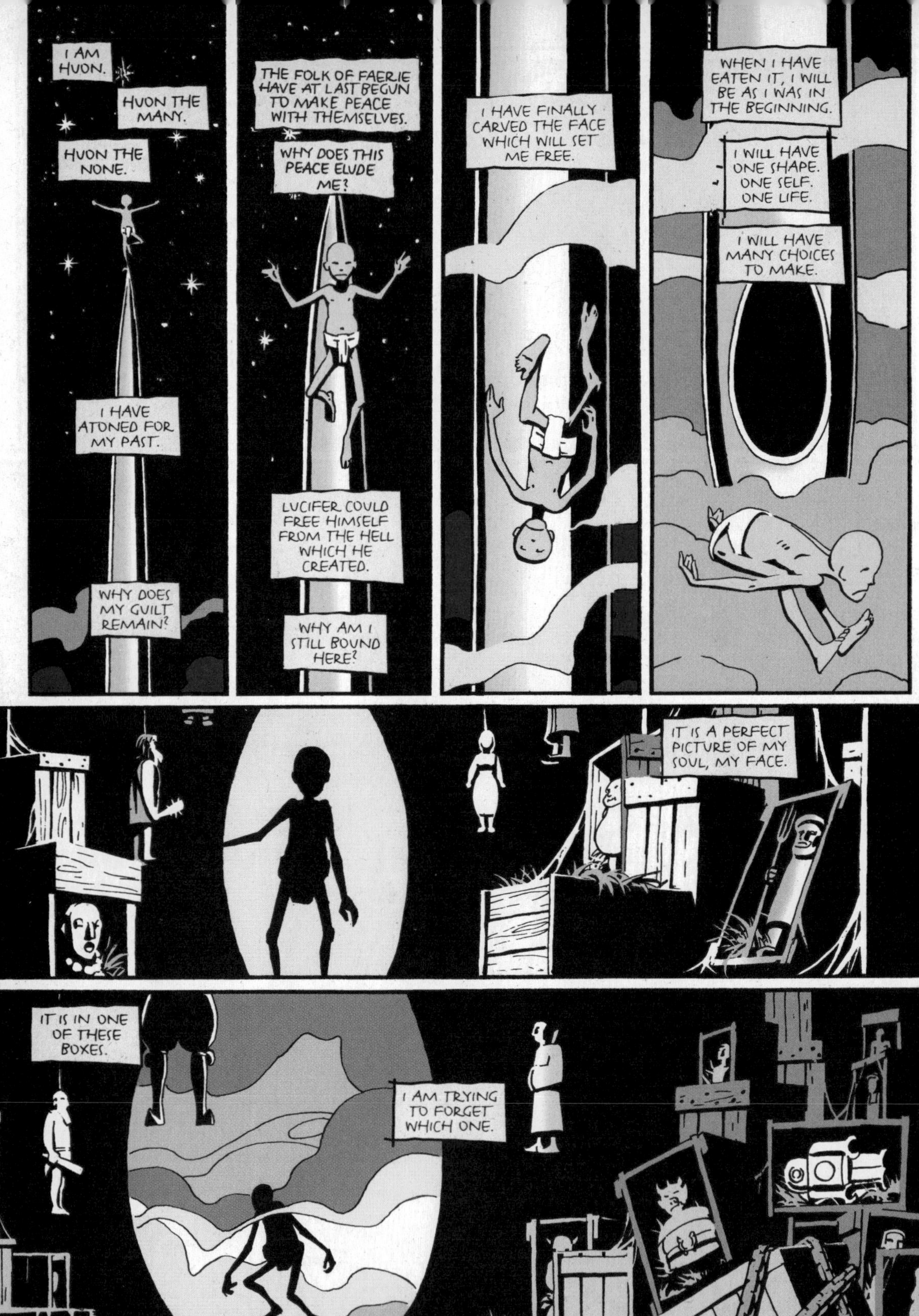

A WORLD of ONE

Timothy Hunter & The Books of Magic Created by Neil Gaiman & John Bolton

Rites of Passage: Conclusion

John Ney Rieber - writer Peter Snejbjerg - artist

Sherilyn van Valkenburgh - colors Richard Starkings & Comicraft/LA - letters

Neil Gaiman - consultant Julie Rottenberg - editor

END

Young Timothy Hunter, destined to become the world's greatest mage, left England hoping to escape the sorcerous and personal woes that plagued him there. During his travels, however, his ex-girlfriend Molly was lured to Faerie, where she was cursed by Queen Titania. Now, although still plagued by the curse, Molly has been granted permission to return to Earth…
L APPEARANCE
GING GARDEN
ARGENT LAKE MINNESOTA.
BUT WHAT ABOUT --
MOLLY.
SHE WAS THERE, I KNOW SHE WAS...
BUT I DIDN'T EVEN GET TO SEE HER.
Oh, GREAT. MUTANT HOUSING.
I'M NOT EVEN IN FAERIE ANYMORE.
THINGS DON'T FALL APART THERE.
THEY JUST, Um --
GOD.
WHAT IS THIS?

PHOENIX
THAT'S SO WEIRD.
WHAT ARE THEY DOING IN THERE?
THEY'RE ALL SPRINGY GOING IN, AND ALL CRUMPLED COMING OUT...
THEY'RE GAMBLERS, TWERP.

THE HAPPY ONES HAVEN'T PLAYED YET.
THE SAD ONES HAVE.
Solitaire
JOHN NEY RIEBER writer
PETER GROSS artist
SHERILYN VAN VALKENBURGH colors
RICHARD STARKINGS & COMICRAFT/LA letters
NEIL GAIMAN consultant
JULIE ROTTENBERG editor
Timothy Hunter & The Books of Magic created by Neil Gaiman and John Bolton

SO WHAT'S WITH THE DO NOT DISTURB SIGN, Uh...
Uh-Oh.

WHAT'S THE STORY THIS TIME?
YOU AND THE STRANGER DOING THE ARMAGEDDON TANGO AGAIN?
TALA --
I'M ATTEMPTING TO PERFORM A VERY DEMANDING RITUAL, HERE, SO --

TRY TURNING THAT GEEKY SUIT OF HIS...
...INTO SOMETHING BLACK LEATHER.

THAT SHOULD TAKE THE HOLY WATER OUT OF HIS BALLOON.

Oh NOOO...
I'M GOING TO KILL HIM.
I'M GOING TO WRING HIS TURTLE NECK --

ALL RIGHT. WHEN WAS HE HERE --
AND WHAT WAS HIS EXCUSE THIS TIME --?

TALA --

TANNARAK... HE RUINED THE DÜRER.

MY FAVORITE.

THE ONE OF YOU SMILING.

TALA --
OKAY, OKAY --
I'LL STAY OUT OF IT.
YOU'RE BETTER AT THE TWISTED-VENGEANCE THING THAN I AM, ANYWAY.
TANNY...
WHY DIDN'T HE SMASH THIS ONE, TOO?
THAT'S NOT LIKE THE STRANGER.
HE'S SO OBSESSIVE-COMPULSIVE THAT HE CONSECRATES HIS --
TALA --
TAKE THE PICTURE, AND GET OUT.
GET ON WITH YOUR LIFE.

SLAM
TANNY, YOU CAN'T KEEP ME IN THE DARK ANYMORE.
I KNOW SOMETHING'S WRONG. LET ME HELP.

ARE YOU AFRAID YOU'LL SCARE ME AWAY, IS THAT IT?
YOU SHOULD KNOW ME BETTER THAN THAT.

I'M A QUEEN OF EVIL --
OR HAVE YOU FORGOTTEN?

WE DON'T SCARE.
TAP
TAP
TAP

Oh, TALA...

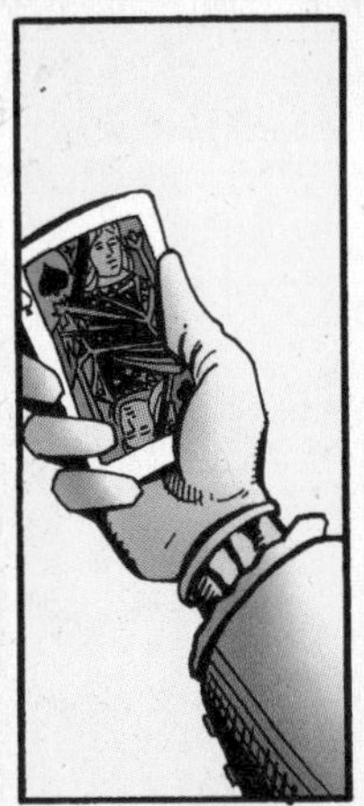

IF ONLY I COULD BELIEVE THAT.

BUT I KNOW YOU, QUEEN OF SHADOWS...

TOO WELL.

MOLLY!
I FOUND YOUR THERMOS FLASK.
IN FAERIE. IN THE FOG.
BUT --
TIM --
THE NEXT PERSON WHO SAYS A WORD TO ME ABOUT FAERIE OR MAGIC IS GOING TO BE SORRY FOR DAYS.
YEARS POSSIBLY.
ARGENT LAKE
1936
BUT YOU CAN BABBLE ALL YOU LIKE ABOUT HOW MUCH YOU'VE MISSED ME.
YOU HAVE MISSED ME, HAVEN'T YOU?

-SIGH-

MOLLY, WHAT *IS* IT?
WHAT'S *WRONG?*

I SHOULD HAVE YELLED AT YOU *BEFORE* I KISSED YOU, THAT'S ALL.
I WON'T DO A PROPER JOB OF IT, NOW.
I'M NOT IN THE *MOOD* ANYMORE.

HELLO? ZATANNA?

I JUST WANT TO TALK, OKAY? NO TRICKS...
TRUCE?

HEY, I KNOW I'M USUALLY LYING WHEN I SAY THAT.
BUT YOU CAN TRUST ME THIS TIME, I SWEAR --

ZATANNA?
ARE YOU HERE?

HI, TALA.
NICE HAT.

HOW'S EVIL TREATING YOU THESE DAYS?

LIKE HELL.
CAN WE SIT DOWN SOMEWHERE?
SURE.
FRA
FRAG
100% OR
CARRO

WANT SOME CARROT JUICE? GREAT STUFF WHEN YOU'RE STRESSING.
IT'S AGAINST MY RELIGION.

SO -- WHAT'S UP?
IT'S TANNARAK.
WE'VE BEEN SEEING EACH OTHER.
Ohh, SINCE THE NIGHT YOU BROUGHT THAT BRITISH KID INTO BEWITCHED --

YOU MEAN THE NIGHT YOU TRIED TO KILL HIM?

DON'T LOOK AT ME THAT WAY.
PLEASE.

DO YOU KNOW HOW TERRIFYING YOU ARE TO US?
YOU CREATURES OF THE LIGHT, WITH YOUR PITILESS EYES...

YOU'RE SO QUICK TO JUDGE US...
BUT WHAT DO YOU KNOW OF THE IMPERATIVES OF DARKNESS?
YOU'VE NEVER SEEN PAST THE SHADOWS.

Mmm...
CORRECT ME IF I'M WRONG, BUT AREN'T YOU THE ONE WITH THE PROBLEM?

SO QUIT BASHING MY FLUFFY BUNNY WORLDVIEW.
IT'S ALL THAT'S KEEPING ME FROM STEALING YOUR HAT.

FOUR THOUSAND YEARS...
FOUR THOUSAND YEARS I SERVED YOU --
WORSHIPPED YOU, FILTHY SKULL.
AND THIS --
kaff
THIS IS HOW YOU KEEP YOUR PROMISES TO ME?
TAK
IMMORTALITY.
GODS, I WANTED IT.
WHAT A FOOL I WAS --
TO BELIEVE.

PHOENIX
UH-OH --
THEY'VE GOT SECURITY. MMM...
want to hear about our grandchildren?
we're going to tell you anyway
THEY LOOK LIKE THE SORT OF PEOPLE WHO'D TAKE THEIR GRANDCHILDREN INAPPROPRIATE PLACES. WE'LL GO IN WITH THEM.
UMM...
DO WE KNOW WHERE WE'RE GOING, EXACTLY?
YOU'RE BUYING ME DINNER.
AT THE FIRST RESTAURANT WE SEE.
MOLLY, I CAN'T!
I LOST TOTO.
TOTO?
MY KNAPSACK
IT'S GOT ALL MY STUFF IN IT.
MAYBE I SHOULD TRY CALLING IT.
IT IS SORT OF A DOGGY BAG. IT MIGHT COME --
CALL IT.
The Hanging Garden
Appetizers
Entrees

MONDAY, I FOUND ***THESE.***

IN A SUITCASE, UNDER HIS BED.

NASTY ENCHANTMENTS ON THESE THINGS.
IS HE...
HURT?
KLAK

TANNARAK?
HE'S MADE TOO MANY BARGAINS WITH THE DARK.

Oh, I'M SURE THERE ARE SOME WAYS HE COULD BE INJURED...
BUT I HAVE NO IDEA WHAT THEY MIGHT BE.

I DON'T THINK HE KNOWS EITHER.

SIGH.

I THINK THAT'S WHY HE'S STILL ALIVE.

ARE YOU ENJOYING YOUR LITTLE JOKE?
TAN
WELL, LAUGH WHILE YOU CAN, DEATH-GOD.
BECAUSE YOU'RE AS GOOD AS DEAD NOW, YOU FILTHY SKULL --
KRASH
YOU'VE GOT NOTHING.
NO MORE STATUES, NO MORE TEMPLES...
NO WORSHIPPERS.
NO ONE'S GOING TO BE BOWING DOWN TO YOU NOW.
KRAK
NO ONE'S GOING TO BE BLEEDING FOR YOU.
THE DRINKS...
...ARE NO LONGER ON THE HOUSE.

DO YOU KNOW WHAT YOU'D *LIKE*, OR DO YOU NEED A LITTLE MORE --

WE'RE *VERY* READY TO ORDER.

THIS IS AWFUL.
HAS HE BEEN LIVING HERE?
IF YOU CAN CALL THIS LIVING.
-:Faugh:-
THIS PLACE STINKS OF DEATH.
ROT --

MOLLY --
ARE YOU ALL RIGHT?
NO.
MOLLY, WAIT--
NO!
STAY HERE.

MOLLY!
GOD.
Oh GOD --
BOOM
SHIT.

JUST LIKE UNCLE DONAL.
I...
DOUBT THAT.

CHRIST --
YOU'RE ALIVE.

BUT...

NO.
YOU DIDN'T MISS.

I'M TRYING TO THINK OF A REASON I SHOULDN'T KICK YOU.
THEY WOULDN'T LET ME KICK UNCLE DONAL AFTER HE SHOT HIMSELF.

I WANTED TO LIVE --
SO YOU SHOT YOURSELF?
THAT WAS BRIGHT.
YOU DON'T UNDERSTAND.

I FOUND THE WAY.
I'M GOING TO LIVE FOREVER.

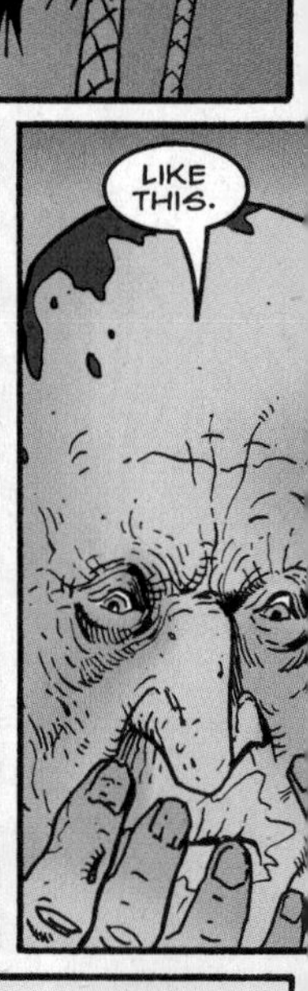
LIKE THIS.

Oh.

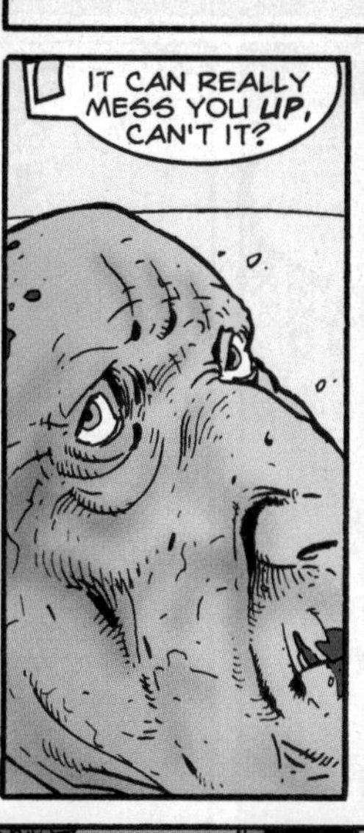
IT CAN REALLY MESS YOU UP, CAN'T IT?

MAGIC.

SO.
IT WASN'T JUST MY EYES.

YOU'RE NOT HUMAN EITHER.

NICE OF YOU TO NOTICE.
NO ONE ELSE HAS.

NOT EVEN MY BOYFRIEND.

TROUBLE WITH THE FAIRIES?
HOW'D YOU GUESS?

WHEN YOU WALK.
YOUR FEET DON'T TOUCH THE GROUND.

ONE OF THE CLASSIC FAIRY CURSES.

I HATE FAIRIES.

I CAN'T EAT REAL FOOD ANYMORE.
NEITHER CAN I. I DON'T HAVE THE TEETH FOR IT.

I CAN'T EVEN DRINK WATER.
EVERY TIME I PICK UP A MARTINI GLASS, I DUMP OLIVES IN MY LAP.

I'D PROBABLY BURST INTO FLAME IF I LOST MY TEMPER.
Heh.
YOU THINK YOU'VE GOT A TEMPER.

YOU SHOULD SEE WHAT I DID TO THE GOD WHO DID THIS TO ME.

AND I JUST WANT TO DIE WHEN I THINK ABOUT SUMMER.

WHAT GOOD IS JULY, IF YOU CAN'T WALK ON THE GRASS AND FEEL IT?

KNOW WHAT I MEAN?

NO.

Oh.
SO HOW OLD ARE YOU, ANYWAY?

THE FIRST SPHINX. THE FIRST ONE.
HAD MY, MY... FACE...

I NEED TO FIND A BATHROOM.

THEN I WANT TO GO OUTSIDE.

MOLLY!
WAIT!
TIM?
TANNARAK.
ASINO

GODS.
LOOK, AT HIS FACE.

TELL HIM I SAID **GOODBYE**, ZATANNA.
TELL HIM NOT TO --
Uh-uh.

TELL HIM YOURSELF.

TALA..?

HI, TANNY.

I WANT TO GO OUTSIDE.

HI, TIM.
WHO'S YOUR FRIEND?
ZATANNA!

ZATANNA, THIS IS MOLLY.
MOLLY --

YOU'RE NOT LISTENING.
NEITHER OF YOU.

SORRY, TIM.
BUT I'LL NEVER FORGIVE MYSELF IF I MISS THIS.

ENOYREVE EDISTUO.

BUT YOU KNOW WHAT'S REALLY WEIRD?
SHE'S OLDER THAN HE IS.

SHE'S NOT GOING TO STAY WITH HIM, IS SHE?

NO.
BUT I WOULDN'T FEEL TOO SORRY FOR TANNARAK.

HE'LL FORGET HER BEFORE SHE FORGETS HIM.
fin

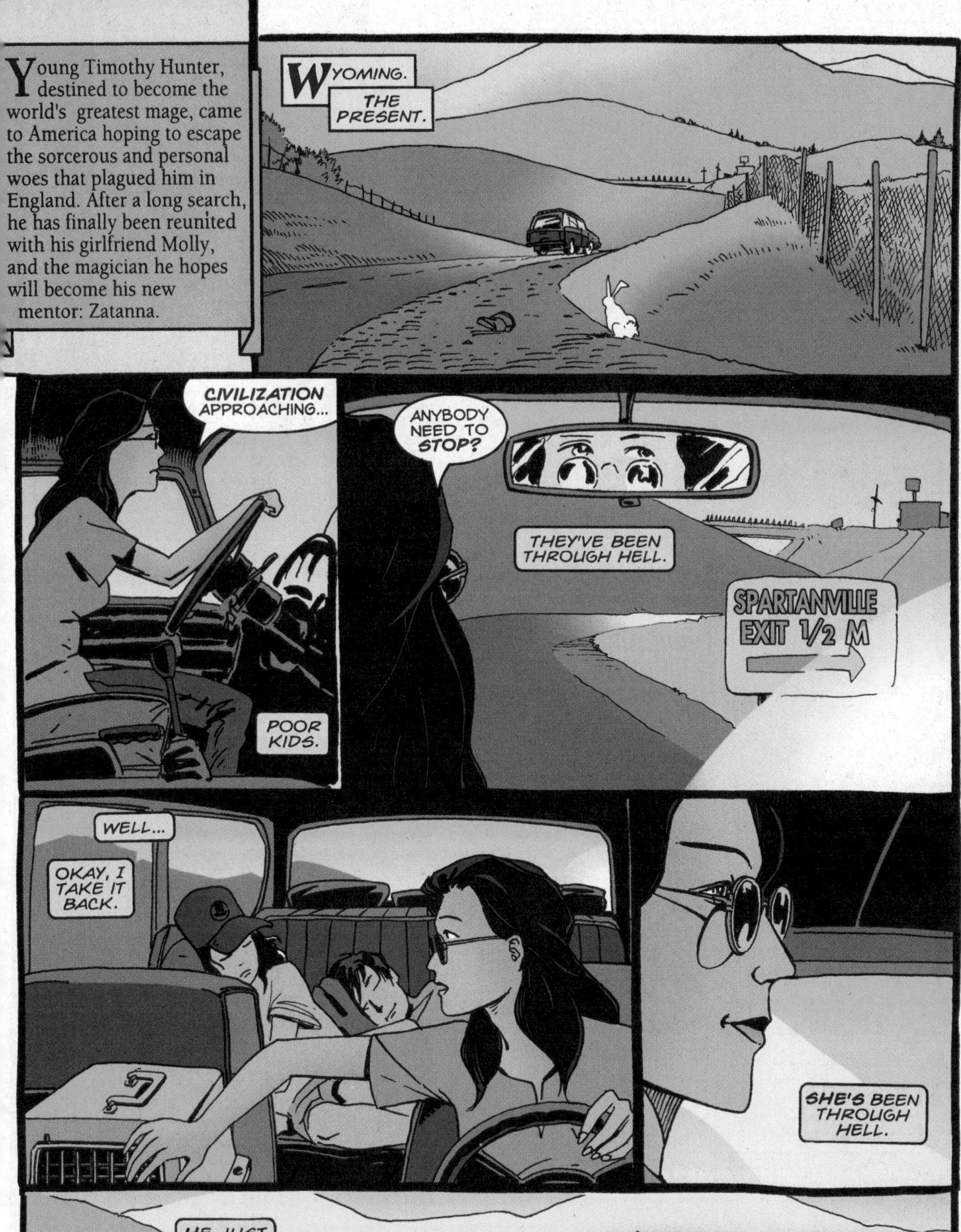
Young Timothy Hunter, destined to become the world's greatest mage, came to America hoping to escape the sorcerous and personal woes that plagued him in England. After a long search, he has finally been reunited with his girlfriend Molly, and the magician he hopes will become his new mentor: Zatanna.
WYOMING.
THE PRESENT.
CIVILIZATION APPROACHING...
POOR KIDS.
ANYBODY NEED TO STOP?
THEY'VE BEEN THROUGH HELL.
SPARTANVILLE EXIT 1/2 M
WELL...
OKAY, I TAKE IT BACK.
SHE'S BEEN THROUGH HELL.
HE JUST THINKS HE HAS.
SPARTANVILLE
NEW SPARTA

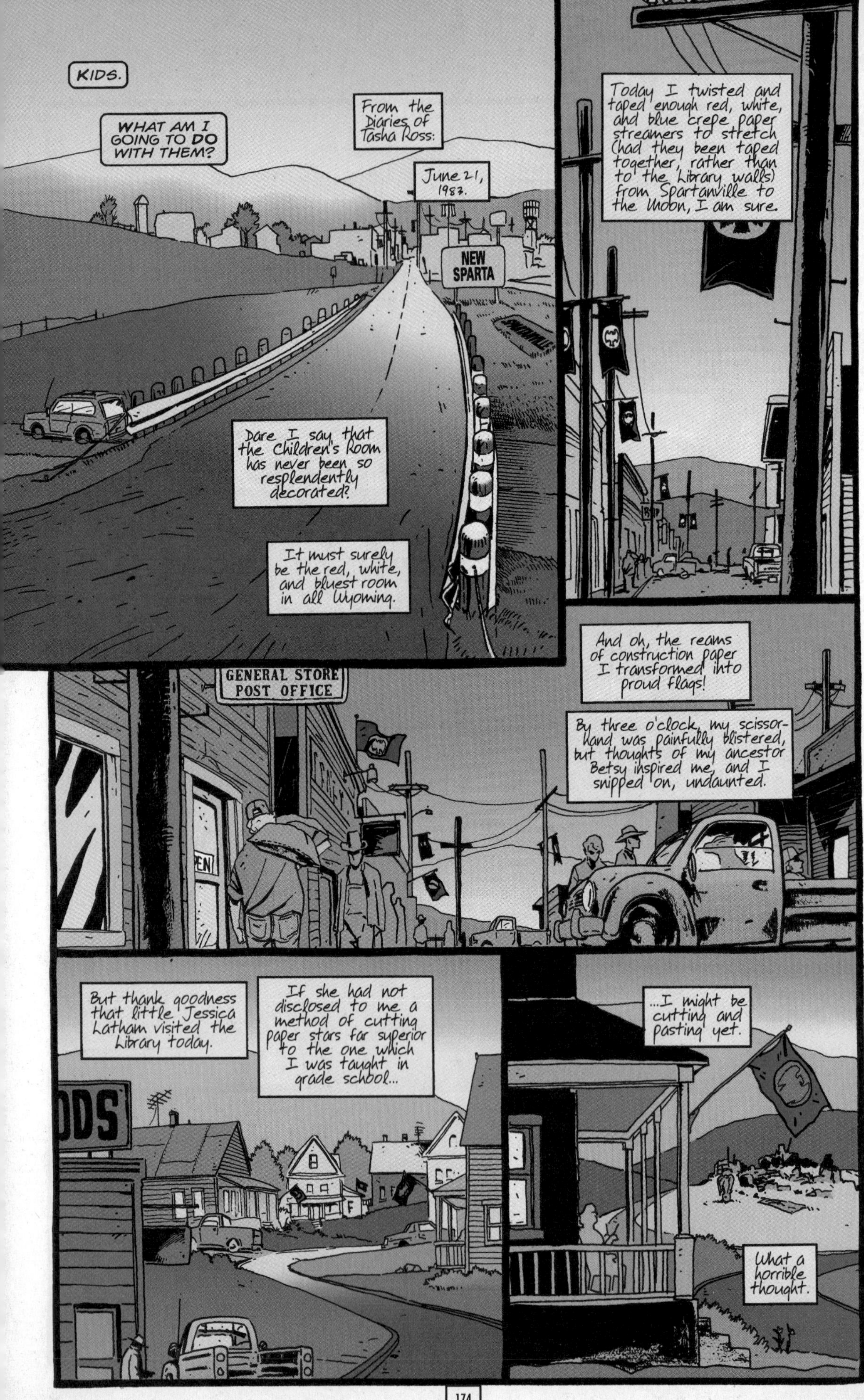

KIDS.
WHAT AM I GOING TO DO WITH THEM?
From the Diaries of Tasha Ross:
June 21, 1983.
NEW SPARTA
Dare I say that the Children's Room has never been so resplendently decorated?
It must surely be the red, white, and bluest room in all Wyoming.
Today I twisted and taped enough red, white, and blue crepe paper streamers to stretch (had they been taped together, rather than to the Library walls) from Spartanville to the Moon, I am sure.
GENERAL STORE
POST OFFICE
And oh, the reams of construction paper I transformed into proud flags!
By three o'clock, my scissor-hand was painfully blistered, but thoughts of my ancestor Betsy inspired me, and I snipped on, undaunted.
But thank goodness that little Jessica Latham visited the Library today.
If she had not disclosed to me a method of cutting paper stars far superior to the one which I was taught in grade school...
...I might be cutting and pasting yet.
What a horrible thought.

Jessica really is a darling child.
PUBLIC LIBRARY
I cannot imagine how her mother could bear to send her away.
But Jessica did inform me today in no uncertain terms that she must live with her grandmother now.
"Mommy's got religion now," she said...
"So she can't have me."
CHILDREN
It seems that Absalom Smith has convinced his flock that no children but his own may enter the Kingdom of Heaven.
HERE TRUTH PREVAILED JULY 4 1983

NEARBY.
THE REST AREA.
AS THE MOUNTAINS BOW BEFORE THE SUN, SO WE ABASE OURSELVES BEFORE THEE, LIBERTY.
WE HAVE BEEN CAST OUT.
WE TURN TO THEE FOR SHELTER.
WE TURN TO THEE.
WE TURN TO THEE.
WE TURN TO THEE.
WE ARE WEAK.
WE TURN TO THEE FOR STRENGTH.
WE TURN TO THEE.
WE TURN TO THEE.
WE TURN TO THEE.
WE TURN TO THEE.
WE TURN TO THEE.
WE TURN TO THEE.

AND WE HUNGER.
THIS DAY, OUR NEED IS GREAT.
FEED US.
The Motherless
John Ney Rieber writer
Peter Gross artist
Sherilyn Van Valkenburgh colors
Richard Starkings & Comicraft /LA--letters
Neil Gaiman consultant
Julie Rottenberg editor
Timothy Hunter and The Books of Magic created by Neil Gaiman and John Bolton.
LIBERTY
Cola
Cola
FEED US.
FEED US.
FEED US.
FEED US.
FEED US.
FEED US.
VRRMMMM
MOTHERLESS!
TRAVELLERS COME.

Uhm --
WHERE ARE WE?
THE MIDDLE OF NOWHERE.
CHRIST, IT'S ALL THE SAME.
AND IT JUST GOES ON AND ON...
NOT REALLY.
BUT IT SURE SEEMS LIKE IT WHEN YOU'RE DRIVING THROUGH.
MOLLY...
WHERE DO YOUR PARENTS THINK YOU ARE?
I DON'T KNOW.

THEY STILL THINK I'M AT GRANNY'S, FOR ALL I KNOW.
IF THEY DIDN'T HAVE TO FEED FILTHY FOR ME, THEY PROBABLY WOULD HAVE FORGOTTEN ALL ABOUT ME BY NOW.
I'VE GOT A HUGE FAMILY.
AND YOUR GRANNY?
SHE'S BOUND TO HAVE NOTICED THAT YOU'VE DISAPPEARED.
Oh, I'M SURE SHE HAS.
SHE'S THE ONE WHO THREW ME TO THE FAIRIES.
Oh.
AND SHE'S FEY.
SHE PROBABLY KNOWS MORE ABOUT WHERE I AM NOW THAN I DO.
Oh.
WELL...
I FEEL SORT OF LIKE AN OGRE FOR BRINGING THIS UP, MOLLY... BUT WE'VE GOT TO TALK ABOUT IT SOMETIME.
SO FAR AS THE LAW IS CONCERNED?
YOU'RE KIDS.
I'M A KIDNAPPER.

SKREEK
YOU SEE THE RED TABLE THERE?
NOT YET.
PLEASE?
I'M NOT READY.
YOU WILL WALK TO THE RED TABLE, SISTER JESSICA, AND YOU WILL PLACE THE UNSANCTIFIED CHILD UPON IT --
PROVING YOUR FAITH.
YOU WILL THEN RETURN TO THE VEHICLE --
WITHOUT LOOKING BACK.

WAAA
WAAA
WAAA
WAAA --
SISTER JESSICA!
WHAT DID I TELL YOU ABOUT LOOKING BACK?
BUT HE --
HE --
REJOICE, SISTER --
VRRMMMM
YOUR SIN HAS BEEN TAKEN AWAY.

From the Diary of Tasha Ross:
July 4, 1983.
When my choice of words offends them, the masked men burn what I write.
This is the essence of history, I understand now.
History is what is left when the fire has died.
The "Purification" of Spartanville is complete.
The followers of the prophet and patriot Absalom Smith rose in the night and swept through the town...
Like a flaming sword.
My life has been spared.
In a matter of hours, the masked men inform me, the Eagle of Truth himself shall tell me why.
KLANG
I am afraid.

BUT YOU'RE TAKING CARE OF US.
HOW COULD THAT BE WRONG?
I DIDN'T SAY IT WAS WRONG.
I SAID IT WAS ILLEGAL.
LOOK, I KNOW THAT THE LAW HAS TO BE THE SAME WHERE YOU'RE FROM.
UNTIL YOU'RE AN ADULT, YOU HAVE TO BELONG TO SOMEONE.
YOUR PARENTS. A LEGAL GUARDIAN.
OR THE STATE.
THAT'S JUST THE WAY IT IS.
REST AREA 2M
YOU DIDN'T MIND HAVING ME AROUND LAST TIME.
YOU WERE LOOKING FOR A PLACE TO HIDE LAST TIME.
NOT A PLACE TO LIVE.
I HAD TO LEAVE HOME, ZATANNA.
YOU SHOULD HAVE SEEN DAD'S FACE.
WHEN HE SAW ME MAGIC...
ZATANNA...
HE WAS SO AFRAID OF ME.

CRUNCH.
THE NEW ONE WILL NEED MILK.
BEFORE DARK?
THE WAY IS SAFER AFTER DARK.
THIS ONE IS VERY YOUNG.
WEIGH HER DANGER AGAINST YOUR OWN, AND DECIDE.
I WILL GO TO THE FARM ON THE EDGE --
AND GET THE CAN-MILK THEY KEEP FOR THE MOTHERLESS CALVES.
GOOD.
GO.
WAFER --
AS MOTHER SAID, THE SOONER, THE BETTER.
IT IS SLOW CLIMBING WITH ONE HAND.
YOU WILL NEED A CRADLE-SLING.
NIBBLE, THE NEW ONE WILL NEED A BED.
I KNOW HOW!
ZESTINE, THE HOME MUST BE CLEAN FOR THE NEW ONE'S NAMING-FEAST.
DONE IN A BLINK.
SLICE --
WHAT DID YOU HARVEST FROM THE JUNKER?
I SAW METAL-FLASH.

IT IS NOTHING THAT CAN BE SHARED.
MOTHER SAID THAT EVERYTHING IS TO BE SHARED.
I NEVER HEARD HER SAY THAT.
HE HAS QUARTERS.
THEY WERE ON THE JUNKER'S DASHBOARD WHEN IT CAME, BUT THEY WERE NOT THERE WHEN IT LEFT.
AND THERE IS SOMETHING ELSE NEW IN HIS POCKET, TOO.
SHOW US, SLICE.
SNIK

DON'T GET ME WRONG, GUYS --
I KNOW THAT THINGS ARE DIFFERENT FOR YOU.
AND I'M NOT SAYING THAT YOU CAN'T STAY WITH ME.
I WANT YOU TO.
BUT IF YOU'RE GOING TO MOVE IN, YOU'RE GOING TO DO IT RIGHT.
TIM -- YOU'RE GOING TO HAVE TO TALK TO YOUR DAD.
I DON'T CARE WHETHER OR NOT HE LIKES WHAT YOU'RE DOING. BUT HE NEEDS TO KNOW THAT YOU'RE NOT LYING DEAD IN A DUMPSTER SOMEWHERE.
AND MOLLY --
MAYBE SHE ALREADY KNOWS, BUT MAYBE ISN'T GOOD ENOUGH.
YOU'VE GOT TO AT LEAST LET YOUR GRANDMOTHER KNOW WHERE YOU ARE.
SOUNDS LIKE IT WOULDN'T HURT IF YOU ASKED HER A FEW--
ZATANNA?
IF REST AREAS HAVE PLUMBING, CAN WE STOP AT THIS ONE?
REST AREA 1/2M

From the Diary of Tasha Ross:
July 5, 1983
Is it mercy?
KLIK
Absalom Smith will allow no children but his own to live in the "Heaven on Earth" he calls New Sparta.
But he is no Herod, he says, to murder infants in cold blood.
The "Unsanctified" children are merely to be cast into the outer darkness" --
Abandoned at the old Welcome Center, fifteen minutes removed from the edge of town.
I may live in safety, the Eagle of Truth has promised, and care for the children...
Provided that I take the utmost care to hide them from the "infidels and mongrels" who pass by.
But should I compromise the security of his Heaven, Smith warns me, one dear to me shall pay the price.
A hostage.
Oh, Jessica --
Little Jessica, I swear --
No harm will come to you because of me.

I DO NOT LIKE IT.
STILL, IT IS METAL.
GIVE IT TO ME. I WILL PUT IT IN A SAFE PLACE.
I NEVER GET TO KEEP ANYTHING!
IT'S NOT FAIR!
I'M THE ONE WHO RAIDS THE JUNKERS --
SLICE!
SINCE YOU HARVESTED THE QUARTERS FOR THE NEW ONE'S NAMING FEAST --
YOU MAY CHOOSE WHAT WE WILL EAT.
FAB.
IT IS NOT HIS PLACE TO CHOOSE.
LIBERTY SPEAKS TO ME.

EVERY DAY WE RENEW OUR PLEDGE TO MOTHER.
WHAT IS THE LAST THING WE SAY, CHIP?
WITH LIBERTY --
SAY IT.
AND JUSTICE --
FOR --
NO.
MOTHER TASHA IS DEAD NOW.
I PLEDGE ALLEGIANCE TO ME.
DID THE EAGLE MAKE A MISTAKE WHEN HE GAVE YOU TO MOTHER TASHA, CHIP?
YOU WANT YOUR LIBERTY TO EAT EVERYONE ELSE'S --
JUST LIKE HE DOES.
I WONDER...
WHOSE CHILD ARE YOU?
MOTHER'S?
WAAA
OR HIS?

THIS IS A WELCOME CENTER?
WELCOME TO WHAT?
WELCOME TO NOWHERE.
IT'S CLOSED. SORRY, KIDS --
RUOK
CLOSED
WAAA
WAAA
IT'S A BABY.
BUT...
OVER HERE.
WAAA
Oh, GOD...

GNIDEELB POTS.
SDNUOW LAEH.
TNOD YRC.
SOMEONE --
IS GOING TO REGRET THIS --
FOR THE REST OF THEIR MISERABLE LIFE.
ZATANNA...
ALL THIS BLOOD...
IT'S NOT THE BABY'S.
NO --
IT IS MINE.

WHAT WERE THE WORDS YOU SAID TO THE NEW ONE?
I WOULD LIKE TO KNOW THEM.
THE PAIN WENT AWAY WHEN YOU SAID THEM.
AND THE BLEEDING STOPPED.
IT WAS ALMOST LIKE BEING WITH MOTHER.
WHEN SHE KISSED THE HURT AND MADE IT BETTER.
Uhh...
IT WASN'T THE WORDS THAT HEALED YOU.
IT JUST SEEMS THAT WAY.
WHY ARE YOU HOLDING THE LITTLE ONE LIKE THAT?
WAAA WAAA
WAAA
HE IS A BABY, NOT A DEAD SQUIRREL.
WAAA
HERE --
BRAVE BOY, BRAVE BOY...
Shhh...

IT'S AMAZING HOW SOME PEOPLE CAN DO THAT.

BABIES SCREAM LOUDER WHEN I PICK THEM UP.

MOLLY. THIS IS AND THAT'S ZATANNA --

I AM CARAMEL.

AND WHAT ON EARTH ARE YOU DOING OUT HERE WITH A BABY?

ALONE IN THE MIDDLE OF NOWHERE?

ALONE?

WHEET

I KNOW YOU ARE NOT EAGLE-SLAVES.

YOU HAVE DARK HAIR. AND YOU ARE KIND.

BUT YOU ARE NOT OF THE FAMILY...

PRETTY PLEASE?
MOTHER WOULD BE ANGRY WITH ME IF SHE KNEW I WAS TALKING TO YOU.
DO YOU THINK SHE WOULD WANT ME TO SHOW YOU OUR HOME?
BUT --
CHRIST.
AND I THOUGHT TIM WAS GOOD AT DISAPPEARING.
WELL, IF THEY THINK I'M GOING TO DISAPPEAR, THEY'VE GOT ANOTHER THINK COMING.
EKAT SU EREHW EHT SDIK--
Oh, COME ON, ZATANNA --
THEY'VE ALREADY GOT A MOTHER.
WHAT WOULD THEY DO WITH ANOTHER ONE?

VERY *FUNNY*.

WELL, IT'S A FUNNY *WORLD*, ISN'T IT?

YOU'RE SO *WORRIED* ABOUT ME AND MOLLY DOING WHAT *OUR* LOONY PARENTS WANT US TO DO.

BUT WHEN *THESE* KIDS TRY TO MIND *THEIR MOM* INSTEAD OF *YOU* --

ALL OF A SUDDEN THE RULES ARE *DIFFERENT*.

ALL YOU CARE ABOUT IS WHAT *YOU* THINK IS RIGHT.

OKAY.

POINT TAKEN.

WELCOME TO NEW SPARTA HEAVEN ON EARTH

From the Diary of Tasha Ross:

July 4, 1996.

This cavern beside the highway, which seemed to me so bleak and miserable a shelter, thirteen long years ago --

How my heart aches at the thought of leaving it now!

But I am not afraid to die. I have found joy and purpose in life--

Surrounded by the love and laughter of my children.

And as I have learned to see the highway and the wilderness of our world through their untarnished eyes...

A great Mystery has been revealed to me.

KLATCH KLATCH

Young Timothy Hunter, destined to become the world's greatest mage, came to America hoping to escape the sorcerous and personal woes that plagued him in England. After a long search, he has finally been reunited with his girlfriend Molly, and the magician he hopes will become his new mentor: Zatanna.

AND UGLY.

NOBODY IS.

BUT ON THESE CROOKED STREETS WHERE THE FOG SLINKS LIKE A *CAT* IN A VETERINARIAN'S *WAITING ROOM* UNTIL THE WIND HOWLS DOWN FROM THE CANYONS LIKE AN *ORTHODONTIST'S BILL* TO DRIVE IT *AWAY*...

YOU GET *TOUGH* OR YOU GET *EATEN.*

EATEN *ALIVE.*

CASE IN POINT.

THE GIRL ANSWERS TO THE NAME OF *MOLLY* --

MOLLY O'REILLY.

SHE DRIFTED INTO TOWN ABOUT A *MONTH* AGO.

TRAVELING WITH SOME PUNK WHO'S SUPPOSED TO BE A REAL HOTSHOT *MAGICIAN*--

THE HOTTEST SINCE *MERLIN,* THEY TELL ME.

MOLLY'S GOT A SECRET.
DAD?
HI.
NOTHING UP MY SLEEVE
TIMOTHY HUNTER & THE BOOKS OF MAGIC CREATED BY NEIL GAIMAN & JOHN BOLTON.
PACIFIC BELL
PARKING ONLY
THIS IS MOLLY. I WANT TO COME HOME.
JOHN NEY RIEBER AND PETER GROSS WRITERS
PETER GROSS ARTIST
SHERILYN VAN VALKENBURGH COLORS
COMICRAFT'S LIZ AGRAPHIOTIS LETTERS
NEIL GAIMAN CONSULTANT
JULIE ROTTENBERG EDITOR
EXAMINER

A FEW BLOCKS AWAY.

NOK NOK

TIM?

-MNPH- GO AWAY.

RISE AND SHINE, SLEEPY-HEAD --

WE'VE GOT A LOT TO DO TODAY.

ZATANNA --

I DON'T KNOW WHAT TIME IT IS IN YOUR WORLD, BUT IN MINE IT'S STILL DARK OUTSIDE.

Hmmm...

AS YOU CAN PLAINLY SEE, I HAVE NOTHING UP MY SLEEVE --

NO MAGICAL APPARATUS OF ANY KIND CONCEALED UPON MY PERSON.

BY THE POWER OF MY WILL ALONE, I WILL TRANSFORM THIS ORDINARY CRYSTAL ORNAMENT --

SALVAGED FROM AN INJURE CHANDELIER ACQUIRED AT YARD SALE LAS OCTOBER --

INTO A TALISMAN OF IRRESISTIBLE SOLAR MAGNETISM!

BEHOLD, SLOTHFUL APPRENTICE --

AT MY COMMAND--
VOILA! DAY BREAKS!
NOW GET YOUR LAZY BUNS OUT OF BED.
I DON'T BELIEVE IT --
THAT'S THE WILDEST THING I'VE EVER SEEN.
HOW DID YOU DO IT, ZATANNA?
YOU DIDN'T TALK BACKWARDS OR ANYTHING!
I COULDN'T EVEN FEEL THE MAGIC HAPPEN...
HOUDINI
-HMPH-
I'LL TEACH YOU THE SPELL, LACKLUSTER APPRENTICE...
IF YOU'RE DOWNSTAIRS FOR BREAKFAST BEFORE YOUR EGGS GET COLD.

LISTENING TO THE GIRL SPILL HER GUTS OVER GOD KNOWS HOW MANY MILES OF TRANSATLANTIC CABLE GOT ME THINKING.
THIRTY YEARS I TOLD MYSELF DANGER WAS MY BUSINESS.
BUT DECEMBER FIFTH, 1949, I WOKE UP IN A FLY-BY-NIGHT MOTEL TO FIND THE UGLY TRUTH STARING ME IN THE FACE LIKE THE MARA-SCHINO CHERRY IN A SHIRLEY TEMPLE.
JACK HAMMER NEVER TOOK CHANCES.
HE KEPT SECRETS.
UNTIL HE HAD MORE SECRETS THAN BLOOD IN HIM.
AND HE WASN'T A MAN ANYMORE.
MORNING.
HI, MOLLY --
CAN I SCRAMBLE YOU SOME EGGS?
NO THANKS.
I FEEL SCRAMBLED ENOUGH THIS MORNING --
ZATANNA --
TOAST, THEN?
NO THANKS.
I'M FEELING PRETTY WELL TOASTED, TOO.
ZATANNA!
ARE YOU GOING TO TELL ME OR AREN'T YOU?

WHAT'S HE ON ABOUT?
THE COMMENCEMENT OF HIS FORMAL MAGICAL EDUCATION.
HE THINKS I MADE THE SUN COME UP AT FIVE-THIRTY-SEVEN TODAY.

DOES HE REALLY?
I'VE BEEN WAITING FOR HIM TO WORK IT OUT.
HE HASN'T QUITE GOT IT, YET.

THAT'S OUR TIM...

WHY AREN'T YOU AT YOUR STATION?
I'VE BEEN LOOKING ALL OVER FOR YOU --
SHHH --

YOUR SHIFT OFFICIALLY ENDED AT SUNRISE.
I SUGGEST THAT YOU RETURN TO THE LIBRARY, AND FILE YOUR REPORT.

JACK?
WHAT'S GOING ON IN THERE?
YOU TELL ME.

WORD IS, THIS HUNTER KID'S AN OPENER.
I --
I AM NOT IN A POSITION TO AFFIRM OR DENY THAT RUMOR AT THE PRESENT TIME.

AND THE IRISH GIRL --
SHE'S HIS OTHER, ISN'T SHE?
AHHH
WHY DO YOU ASK?

YOU'RE FEELING CLEVER THIS MORNING, AREN'T YOU?
NOT PARTICULARLY.
TIM --
SEE WHERE IT SAYS 'SUNRISE' IN BIG BLACK LETTERS?
"SUNRISE..."
"5:37:22 A.M."
SHE KNEW WHAT TIME THE SUN WOULD COME UP.
BUT...
IT HAPPENED JUST WHEN SHE HELD UP THE CRYSTAL --
SHE'S VERY OBSERVANT, TIM.
AND SHE'S GOT A WATCH.
OH DEAR --
OH DEAR --
OH DEAR --
HEAD!

THE OPENER'S OTHER IS --
SHHH.
REALLY. REGINALD --
DO SHOW SOME CONSIDERATION. DARLING.
ARE YOU TRYING TO GIVE US ALL MIGRAINES?
WHISPER. YOU OAF.
AS AMBROSE SUGGESTS. REGINALD --
THE LIBRARY OF SECRETS IS NO PLACE TO BELLOW PROCLAMATIONS.
APPROACH. LITTLE ONE.
CONFIDE IN ME.
CONFIDE?
PLEASE. HEAD --
I SWEAR I'LL NEVER RAISE MY VOICE AGAIN.
I DON'T WANT TO DIE.
DON'T MAKE ME TELL MY SECRET.

YOU MIS-UNDERSTAND ME, LITTLE ONE -- IT IS A CONFIDENCE I REQUIRE OF YOU, NOT THE REVELATION OF YOUR LIFE'S SECRET.
WHY ARE YOU NOT KEEPING VIGIL AS YOU SHOULD BE?
WHERE IS JACK?
I THINK... I THINK JACK WANTS TO BE INVOLVED.
WITH THE SUBJECTS OF THE SURVEILLANCE.
INVOLVED?
INVOLVED?
THIS IS A DIRE ACCUSATION, REGINALD --
HE WOULDN'T DARE!
HE KNOWS WHAT THE CONSEQUENCES WOULD BE.
I DON'T BELIEVE HE CARES.
HE'S CONVINCED THAT THE NEW OPENER IS ABOUT TO LOSE HIS OTHER --
AND THAT THE OPENER IS SO UNSTABLE, HE'LL ATLANTIS CALIFORNIA WHEN HE FINDS OUT.

WE'LL LOSE OUR ROOFS AND NICHES!
WE'LL LOSE THE LIBRARY!
IT WOULDN'T BE THE FIRST TIME THAT ONE OF US HAS LOST A LIBRARY, I HEAR.
I'VE HEARD THAT ONE, TOO.
ARE YOU TRULY FROM ATLANTIS, HEAD?
ISN'T THAT WHERE YOU LOST YOUR WING?
HAVE YOU ALL GONE MAD? WE DO NOT PRY INTO EACH OTHER'S SECRETS.
IT IS THE OPENER AND HIS OTHER WHOSE SECRETS SHOULD CONCERN YOU, NOW.
THE FATE OF THE LIBRARY COULD HINGE UPON THEIR FAINTEST WHISPER.
YOU MUST FIND THEM!
AND SPY AS YOU HAVE NEVER SPIED BEFORE!

HAVE YOU EVER HEARD THE HEAD SHOUT BEFORE?
ONCE.
HE GETS NERVOUS WHEN THERE ARE OPENERS AROUND.
SOMEONE TOLD ME ONCE THAT AN OPENER SANK ATLANTIS.
I HEARD A SECRET DID IT.
I HEARD IT WAS BOTH.
THEY'RE STILL TALKING ABOUT YOU.
MURMURING, ACTUALLY.
I KNOW.
REGINALD --
YOU MUST NOT ALLOW THE O'REILLY GIRL TO LEAVE.
TOO MUCH IS AT STAKE.
NO THANK YOU.
I'M NOT INTERESTED IN COMMITTING SUICIDE THIS WEEK.
BUT YOU MUST!
IF YOU WANT TO INTERFERE WITH THE NATURAL ORDER OF THINGS, YOU CAN DO IT YOURSELF.

THE CASTRO THEATRE.
SO --
TODAY'S LESSON, PART A:
MOST OF WHAT PASSES FOR MAGIC IS SIMPLY MISDIRECTION, TIM --
ON STAGE, YOU MEAN.
CASTRO
OPENING THURSDAY
ZATANNA
ON STAGE, YEAH --
BUT YOU'LL SEE A LOT OF IT IN JOHN-CONSTANTINE-LAND, TOO...
IF YOU KNOW WHAT TO LOOK FOR.
IF I SUCCEED IN DIRECTING YOUR ATTENTION TO MY SLEEVE --
BY TELLING YOU THERE'S NOTHING UP IT, FOR INSTANCE, WHICH SUGGESTS TO YOU THAT SOMETHING COULD BE --
THEN YOU'RE SO BUSY LOOKING FOR THE RABBIT YOU THINK I MIGHT HAVE HIDDEN UP MY SLEEVE --
HEY, GUYS --
HEY, ZEE.
THAT YOU DON'T NOTICE THE WATCH I'M WEARING.

WHICH BRINGS US TO PART B OF TODAY'S LESSON:
A LOT OF THE TIME, WHEN WE SEE MAGIC --
IT'S BECAUSE WE WANT TO...
NOT BECAUSE IT'S THERE.
WHOOF.
WHAT A DAY.
WOULD YOU KIDS MIND TAKING THE BUNNIES UP TO THE ROOF TO CATCH SOME RAYS?
THEY'RE A LOT EASIER TO HANDLE WHEN THEY'RE HOPPED OUT.
SURE.
SEE YOU...
LATER.
WHAT WAS THAT GLITTERY STUFF SHE GAVE YOU?
GLITTER.
WAS IT FOR THE SHOW?
SHE DIDN'T GIVE ME ANY --
WOW --

THAT MAKES SENSE.
WHAT?
ALL THESE GARGOYLES.
LURKING ON TOP OF A THEATRE.

THEY AREN'T REALLY ALIVE.
THEY JUST LOOK LIKE IT, FROM A DISTANCE.

LIKE THEY'RE IN A REALLY LONG, REALLY SLOW PLAY.
DO YOU KNOW WHAT I MEAN?

THIS ONE'S GOT SPANISH MOSS GROWING IN ITS EARS.
IT PROBABLY DOESN'T USE THEM.

RUN, BUNNIES --
HOP. SCAMPER.
IT'S PROBABLY A BOY.
I'VE SEEN THEM COME AND I'VE SEEN THEM GO --

AND IT WAS CLEAR AS A YOUNG REPUBLICAN'S *COMPLEXION* THAT THIS RELATIONSHIP WAS SO TERMINALLY ON THE SKIDS THAT IT HAD JUMPED THE *RAIL*.

I WISH THEY'D HURRY UP AND GET TO THE SECRETS.

BUTTON YOUR *LIP*, MONKEY BOY.

HE WASN'T TALKING TO HER.

HE WASN'T LISTENING.

SHE WASN'T *REAL* TO HIM ANYMORE.

IT WAS STARTING TO GET TO ME.

THINGS LIKE *ME* ARE LOOKING OVER MY *SHOULDER*.

IT MAKES ME *UNCOMFORTABLE*.

WHO CARED WHAT THE GIRL WAS GOING THROUGH?

THE *HEAD*?

REGGIE AND THE BOYS?

NO *WAY*, JOSE.

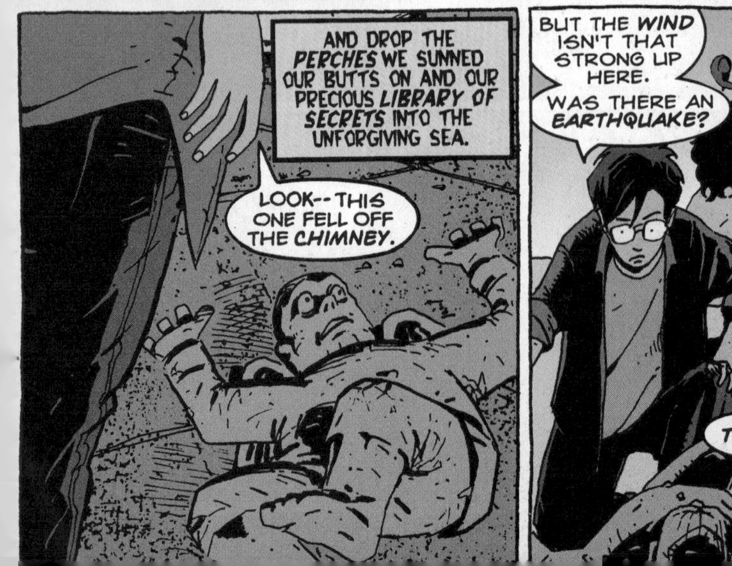

I SHOVED MONKEY BOY OFF THE CHIMNEY.

ARE YOU BOYS TAKING NOTES?
THIS IS NO SECRET. BUT I WANT IT ON THE RECORD ANYWAY. YOU HEAR ME?

I GAVE REGINALD THE DIRT BATH...
BECAUSE SELF-ABSORBED NIMRODS GET ON MY NERVES.

YOU WITH ME SO FAR --
NIMROD?
HEY --

YOU SEE THESE DEADBEATS FEIGNING STATUESQUE IMMOBILITY?

I'D BOOT THEM OFF THEIR PERCHES, TOO. ONLY I DON'T KNOW WHERE TO START.
WITNESSES. THEY CALL THEMSELVES -- GUARDIANS OF SECRETS.
BUT THE TRUTH IS, THEY'RE JUST --

SECRETS?
DID YOU SAY SECRETS?

WELL, YOU WON'T FIND ANY HERE.

SO I GUESS YOU FINALLY TOLD YOUR GIRL ABOUT THAT LITTLE CAMPING TRIP YOU WENT ON?
WITH THE SUCCUBUS. THE BLONDE.

YOU WENT CAMPING WITH LEAH?
WHEN?
UHH... WHEN I FIRST GOT HERE.
SHE PICKED ME UP BY ACCIDENT. AT THE AIRPORT.
I'LL SAY SHE PICKED YOU UP.
WHAT WAS THAT SUPPOSED TO MEAN?
WE JUST WENT CAMPING.
THAT'S ALL.
ON JULY THE SIXTH AT ROUGHLY 11:23 P.M. ALLEATHA CLIMBED INTO YOUR SLEEPING BAG --
WEARING YOUR FACE, MOLLY.
AFTER APPROXIMATELY THIRTEEN MINUTES OF AWKWARD CLINCHING, YOU PENETRATED THE DECEPTION AND PUSHED HER AWAY.
SIX SECONDS BEFORE MIDNIGHT, YOU HAD HER TONGUE IN YOUR MOUTH AGAIN.

YOU WANTED SECRETS, OPENER?

TRY THAT ONE ON FOR SIZE.

IT'S TRUE.
THAT'S WHAT HAPPENED.

BUT MOLLY WAS RUNNING AROUND WITH THAT FAIRY HORSE-PRINCE GUY --

TAIK.

YEAH --
YOU KNOW ALL ABOUT TAIK, DON'T YOU, NIMROD?

BECAUSE I TOLD YOU.

WELL...
I DON'T LIKE BEING FAIR, BUT I SUPPOSE I SHOULD BE.

IF I HAVE ANY SECRETS THAT WRETCHED, GO ON --

TELL TIM.

I WISH I DID HAVE SOME DIRTY DIRT ON YOU, KID.
A LITTLE SHOCK TREATMENT MIGHT BE JUST WHAT THE DOCTOR ORDERED.
BLOW THE DUST OUT OF YOUR BOY'S HEAD.

BUT I DON'T EVEN KNOW IF WHAT I GOT ON YOU QUALIFIES AS A SECRET.
GO ON...
YOU GONNA TELL THE NIMROD HERE WHY YOU'RE LEAVING, OR ARE YOU JUST TAKING OFF?
WHAT?

MOLLY'S LEAVING?
WHY NOT? YOU DON'T LISTEN TO ME --
MUCH LESS TALK TO ME.
BUT --
DON'T TOUCH ME.

NOTHING'S REAL TO YOU NOW...
UNLESS IT'S SHINY AND NEW AND MAGIC.
THAT'S NOT TRUE --
ISN'T IT?

WHEN I CAME BACK FROM FAERIE, YOU DIDN'T EVEN NOTICE THAT I COULDN'T WALK ON THE GROUND ANYMORE.
I DON'T GO AROUND STARING AT PEOPLE'S FEET.

NO, I SUPPOSE YOU DON'T.
I DON'T SUPPOSE YOU NOTICE WHO'S NOT HAVING BREAKFAST OR LUNCH OR DINNER WITH YOU, EITHER.

OR ICE CREAM.

I CAN'T EAT REAL FOOD ANYMORE.
IT MAKES ME SICK.

I HAVE TO EAT FAIRY FOOD.

IT SUCKS, TIM.
LIKE LEAH SAYS -- TOTALLY.

IT WOULD HAVE BEEN WORTH IT IF I'D FOUND YOU WHEN I FOUND YOU.
I THOUGHT I HAD.
DON'T BE LIKE THIS, MOLLY -- PLEASE!
WE'RE TALKING NOW, AREN'T WE?

BUT IT'S LIKE ZATANNA SAID --

I'M LISTENING TO YOU --

SOMETIMES WHEN YOU SEE MAGIC --
IT'S NOT BECAUSE IT'S THERE.

IT'S BECAUSE YOU WANT TO SEE IT.

GOOD-BYE, TIM.

MOLLY, WAIT --
I WAITED, TIM.
I DID.
THERE'S NO PLACE LIKE HOME...THERE'S NO PLACE LIKE HOME...
I'D DONE IT.
I'D BROKEN EVERY RULE IN THE BOOK OF SECRETS, AND I'D BE FOUR HUNDRED POUNDS OF GRAVEL OR DUST OR WORSE BY SUNRISE. BUT THAT WAS OKAY BY ME.
MAYBE I'D DOOMED THE LIBRARY OF SECRETS AND MAYBE I HADN'T. MAYBE I'D DOOMED CALIFORNIA.
I COULD LIVE WITH THAT.
FOR THE FIRST TIME IN MY LIFE, I KNEW I'D DONE THE RIGHT THING FOR A HALFWAY HUMAN REASON.
THE GIRL WASN'T ABOUT TO BACK OUT NOW, OR FEEL GUILTY ABOUT LEAVING TIMMY THE NIMROD BEHIND.
SHE WASN'T GOING TO WAKE UP ONE MORNING TO FIND A GODAWFUL STONE FACE STARING BACK AT HER FROM THE MIRROR.
SHE WAS GOING TO BE OKAY.
Oh, GOD...
WELL, THAT'S ONE CONSOLATION.
IF THE PENINSULA GOES DOWN, SHE WON'T BE ON IT.

ZATANNA SENT HER HOME.
ZATANNA.
WHY DIDN'T ANYONE TELL ME?
A WORD IN YOUR EAR. NIMROD --
BEFORE I GO CRUMBLY OR SHATTER OR DO WHATEVER IT IS WE DO WHEN WE BREAK THE RULES --
YOU KNOW WHERE GARGOYLES COME FROM?
I DON'T KNOW AND I DON'T CARE.
YOU SHOULD.
WE'RE PEOPLE.
PEOPLE WHO CHOKED BACK ONE SECRET TOO MANY.

PEOPLE WHO PLAYED IT SAFE.
NIMRODS LIKE YOU.
LADIES AND GENTLEMEN --
AS YOU CAN SEE, I HAVE NOTHING UP MY SLEEVE BUT BIRDS --
OOPS...
DRAT.
POP
DON'T YOU JUST HATE IT WHEN THAT HAPPENS --
CAGES POPPING UP WHERE BIRDS SHOULD BE?
Mmmm...
NOW, IF I COULD HAVE A VOLUNTEER FROM THE AUDIENCE?
"TO OPEN A WINDOW?
"AND LET THE POOR THINGS OUT?"
END

Cover 33

Cover 34

Cover 35

Cover 36

Cover 37

Cover 38

Cover 39

Cover 40

Cover 41